A.K. Macdougall was born in Melbourne in 1943 and entered book publishing in 1964. He has published under the Clarion imprint since 1969. Among the numerous books he has written is *Anzacs: Australians at War* (1991), which is currently in its third edition. He was Editor-in-Chief of *The Australian Encyclopaedia*, 6th Edition (1996).

War Letters
of
General Sir John Monash

Edited with an Introduction
by A.K. Macdougall

Duffy & Snellgrove
Sydney

Published by Duffy & Snellgrove in 2002
PO Box 177 Potts Point NSW 1335 Australia
info@duffyandsnellgrove.com.au

War Letters of General Monash, edited by F.M. Cutlack,
first published Sydney, 1934

Distributed by Pan Macmillan

Cover design by Alex Snellgrove
The image of Monash on the cover of this book
comes from the Australian War Memorial neg # E2750
Rising Sun badge courtesy of
Army Headquarters, Canberra
Typeset by Cooper Graphics
Printed by Griffin Press

ISBN 1 876631 27 9

visit our website: www.duffyandsnellgrove.com.au

CONTENTS

Introduction

When the *War Letters of General Monash* was first published one British reviewer, Edmund Blunden, author of the classic *Undertones of War*, wrote (in 1935): 'I should not be surprised if these letters gained the reputation of being the best penned by any soldier of similar rank and sphere. Monash was able to think of the war not only as a problem for the intellect but also as a destiny that was shaking the chateau windows and shattering the face of things.'

Monash was possibly the only true intellectual among the senior commanders of World War I. A university graduate in three faculties, he was a richly cultured human being, a successful businessman and part-time soldier before he rose in just two years from commanding a brigade to leading an entire corps to victory on the Western Front. He was able to observe all around him with a detachment and objectivity rare in a senior soldier, and record his impressions vividly, as if he were writing not for his family and friends but for posterity. Music was one of his joys, engineering his profession, and he would describe war not as a game or as sport – favoured metaphors of British generals – but as a problem of engineering. And once in a famous passage he likened it to a score in an orchestral composition 'where the various arms and units are the instruments, and the tasks they perform are their respective musical phrases ... controlled to an exact time-table'.

Monash's wartime letters provide a remarkable self portrait. Written to his wife Victoria and intended only for her eyes and their daughter's, they are extraordinarily candid considering the military information and criticisms they contain. It is known that the writer was later cautioned to be more circumspect, and noticeable that in the later years Monash censors himself more rigorously.

Monash's letters have been widely quoted for generations in many histories of the war. They are not only lucid but historically important, for Monash was close to the central drama of the war from the moment he sailed with the first convoys of Australians in 1914, a colonel who had never heard a shot fired in anger, to the days of his astonishing victories in France in 1918, when he showed a mastery of the art of war that places him among the outstanding Allied military commanders in a conflict in which few had shone.

So remarkable was the success of the Australian Corps under his command that Monash was spoken of as the man whom Prime Minister Lloyd George would have chosen to replace the stolid, unimaginative Haig as Commander-in-Chief of the British Armies in France had the war continued into 1919. The British Prime Minister's description of him is well known: 'Unfortunately the British Army did not bring into prominence any commander who, taking him all round, was more conspicuously fitted for the post [than Haig]. No doubt Monash would, if the opportunity had been given him, have risen to the height of it, but the greatness of his abilities was not brought to the attention of the Cabinet ... Professional soldiers could hardly be expected to advertise the fact that the greatest strategist in the Army was a civilian when the war began ... Monash was, according to the testimony of those who knew well his genius for war and what he accomplished by it, the most resourceful General in the whole of the British Army.' Lloyd George's words were written in 1936 and his contempt for Haig's abilities erodes some of the value of this tribute to the Australian general, but other authorities have confirmed Monash's high reputation. The British military theorist and historian Liddell Hart wrote in an obituary of Monash: 'He had probably the greatest capacity for command in modern war among all those who held command [in the 1914-18 War] ... His views were as large as his capacity.' Field-Marshal Lord Montgomery of Alamein wrote in 1968: 'I would name Sir John Monash as the best general on the Western Front in Europe; he possessed real creative originality, and the war might well have been over sooner, and certainly with fewer casualties, had Haig been relieved of his command and Monash appointed to command the British Armies in his place.'

Yet for nearly fifty years no biography of Monash existed. Readers interested in his life inevitably turned to the volume of his wartime letters edited by one of his former officers, Frederick Cutlack (the work from which this volume has been drawn), and to Monash's own book, *The Australian Victories in France in 1918*, published in 1920. It was an English writer, A.J. Smithers, who first attempted a biography (*Sir John Monash*, 1973), relying principally on published sources. Yet Monash still remained unknown, as impressive and intimidating as his bronze equestrian statue that stands in the Domain near Melbourne's Shrine of Remembrance. Monash's personal papers remained closed. A prospective biographer faced a formidable task, for the General's letters (both written by him and to him) alone numbered 70,000 items. In 1975, however, Monash's descendants made available to the historian Geoffrey Serle all of Sir John's private papers, with no conditions attached to their use. The resulting work, *John Monash: A Biography*, published in 1982, is possibly the finest biography of a public figure and private man published in Australia. It has been drawn on in the preparation of this edition of Monash's own vivid account of his war.

★

For a prominent military commander, John Monash came from the unlikeliest of backgrounds. He was a Jew from a family of scholars and merchants long settled in Krotoszyn, in the Posen (Poznan) province of Prussian-ruled Poland, not far from Breslau (Wroclau). His grandfather, Baer-Lobel Monasch, was a printer and publisher of learned works in Hebrew and German. His father, Louis Monasch, migrated to Australia in 1854 during the gold rush and set up in Melbourne as an importer and commission agent. On returning to Europe on business, Louis married a Jewess, Bertha Manasse, in Stettin in 1863. The couple's first child and only son, John, was born in Dudley Street, West Melbourne, on 27 June 1865. Two daughters were also born: Mathilde in 1869 and Louise in 1873.

After a short period in Jerilderie, where Louis Monash (as he now spelt his name) had opened a store, John returned to Melbourne with his mother and sisters and in 1877 entered Scotch College, Melbourne's most progressive school. He was a day boy, living with his mother and sisters at various homes in and near Richmond while his father attempted to make a success of his country store.

John Monash's childhood was happy. He was precociously intelligent and grew up speaking and reading both English and German, with a love of literature, art and music (he played a piece on the piano for his father when he was six). Shy of sport, he excelled in Scotch College's tough regimen of study – including Latin, Greek, French and the sciences. The city's few Jews were mostly assimilated and in Australia anti-Semitism was almost unknown. In London at war's end in 1918, lionised as the victorious general who had broken the Hindenburg Line, Monash was to explain in a speech: 'In Australia, the land of my birth, perhaps in a higher degree than any other country in the world, there has been throughout, at any rate in my life, never a vestige of discrimination against any one class or creed' and spoke of 'the equality of opportunity which the democracy to which I belong offers to every man and woman regardless of social or religious considerations'. He attended his bar mitzvah at the age of thirteen, but thereafter seldom attended synagogue, even after his marriage. Dark and good-looking, 'a studious, quiet boy', as one contemporary remembered him, he was, in Geoffrey Serle's words, 'a favourite child, an only son with adoring younger sisters, who eventually would stride confidently through life and be attractive to women'. In his last year at Scotch College he was equal dux, shared the *Argus* prize and won the mathematics exhibition with first class honours.

In 1881 Monash went on to the University of Melbourne to study arts, a three-year course, intending to then study engineering. It would be fourteen years before he graduated. Melbourne was then Australia's commercial heart, its largest and most cosmopolitan city. An unparalleled building boom was altering its appearance as commercial buildings, town halls, theatres, art galleries, libraries, churches, mansions and terrace homes rose in the place of modest dwellings, conferring on the city the high Victorian elegance it possesses still. Monash discovered the pleasures of the theatre and concerts and attended talks on religion and philosophy instead of university lectures, enjoying a lively social life while taking himself to task in his diary for this failure to apply himself to study. He welcomed the freedom of thought and the progressive spirit in Melbourne and chided his cousin, Leo Monash in the United States, for espousing pan-Germanism – at a time when German power was growing and Germany's culture was regarded as a model for France and England. 'What,' he asked, 'is there to induce me to cling to the German language and German customs, or to saturate myself in the German spirit?' In 1883 he joined the university company of the Victorian Rifles – the modest beginning of his military career – and the following year was a founder of the university union and editor of the university *Review*. Constantly distracted from his studies and deeply depressed by the loss of his beloved mother to cancer in 1885, Monash took a job as a contracting engineer with David Munro, whose company was then building the graceful Princes Street Bridge over the Yarra River. In this new occupation Monash discovered practical skills: he made working drawings, supervised the cutting of stone and the building of coffer dams, and became experienced at constructing bridges and railway lines. It was the foundation of his career as a civil engineer. In 1891 he took out his BCE (his Arts degree still eluded him). He was now a lieutenant in the Garrison Artillery but had little time for matters military, for in April 1891 he married Victoria (Vic) Moss, who also came from a Jewish family; their daughter Bertha (Bert) was born in 1892. He was always ambitious and shortly afterwards wrote to his wife: 'I will have to choose sooner or later, between my military work and my business career … one of the chief attractions which the military has for me is the social opportunities which it has given, and will in the future give you.'

His marriage and his engineering partnership with Josh Anderson, begun in 1894, coincided with the outset of the economic depression that was to last more than a decade, almost destroy Monash's financial security, and place great strains on his personal happiness. He was constantly travelling, sometimes as far as Western Australia and Queensland, as a contractor or consultant on civil engineering. His health remained robust but his wife's was precarious and he had taken on the care of impecunious relatives. He took special concern in the welfare of his two sisters, Mat, who never married, and Lou, who married a Melbourne metallurgist, Walter Rosenhain, in 1901. In 1900 Monash wrote to a friend: 'I am beginning to feel severely the strain of constant work, and the responsibility of keeping up two households ... If I had only had capital to start with I might have done well but there is fearful competition in contracting work.' He was deeply in debt and dreaded his debts being called in.

Reinforced concrete arrived at an opportune time, just as economic conditions in Australia were improving. A combination of cement and steel rods, it was developed by Monier for the production of flower pots, and was not only cheap but found to have remarkable strength and durability, suitable for the largest of constructions. In 1901 Monash & Anderson entered a partnership with the wealthy contractor David Mitchell, Nellie Melba's father, in the Monier Pipe Co. of Victoria Pty Ltd, and four years later Monash amicably dissolved his partnership with Anderson and became superintending engineer of a new company, Reinforced Concrete and Monier Pipe, working on commission and with a share in the profits. With the renewal of economic activity and construction, these profits soon became substantial. Monash confessed to a friend: 'By dint of hard work and the assistance of influential friends [I] have placed my business in a condition which is now safe from the possibility of ruin. For 2 years it has been touch and go, and any undue pressure by an impatient creditor would have smashed the thing to pieces.' From 1906 Monash knew financial security and – in his biographer's words – became a pillar of Melbourne society, living in affluence, a member of the best clubs, accepted by those whose attentions he respected. And in 1908 he achieved the rank of lieutenant-colonel in the militia and was posted to the Intelligence Corps. Melbourne *Punch* mocked his unmilitary appearance and he had enough sense of humour to take the teasing in good grace. His girth had expanded with his prosperity. He was concerned about his health; he was overworked and overweight, and was – as he remained – a heavy smoker. He and his wife afforded themselves their first overseas holiday, a round the world trip in 1910. He visited England and France, his relatives in Germany, the classic sites of Rome, but Europe itself seems to have left him cold. He loved, however, the energy and mood and pace of the United States. 'America was a most fascinating, stimulating and wonderful experience,' he wrote to a friend. 'New York puts London and Berlin in the shade. The country, the people, the cities, the industry, the organizations and achievements … Are far in advance of anything we have read or understood.'

Responding to pressure from Great Britain on the Dominions to play a stronger role in imperial defence, Australia in 1911 introduced compulsory military training for young men up to twenty-five years old, and launched her own navy; the Royal Military College was opened at Duntroon near Canberra, and in the following year a flying corps was established. By 1913 Monash was – in modern terms – a millionaire, with a mansion in Toorak and numerous other properties. His militia career, however, was in the doldrums. He was still a lieutenant-colonel and was flattered when he was offered command of the 13th Infantry Brigade, which was based in Melbourne's southern suburbs. It was a large command – almost a miniature division – and grew to comprise five infantry battalions (instead of the usual four) in addition to two batteries of artillery, a survey company, an ambulance and an army service corps unit. Monash was angry at the delay in his promotion to colonel (an even higher rank, brigadier-general, was the appropriate one for a command of that size) and was cautioned to be patient by a young friend, Captain Julius Bruche: 'Remember you may be a "hell of a fellah" but you have never yet commanded a battalion or any body of troops in the field. So it is a compliment selecting you.' Most of the battalion commanders were not on speaking terms with each other and absenteeism among the other ranks was rife. But in the manoeuvres held near Lilydale north of Melbourne in February 1914, the newly promoted Colonel Monash's brigade performed well under the gaze of the governor-general and the visiting inspector-general of British overseas forces, Sir Ian Hamilton. The heat was terrible and bushfires burned on the surrounding hills, like battle smoke. Hamilton was impressed by Monash's address to his officers: 'I was prepared for intelligent criticism but I thought they would be so wrapped up in the cotton wool of politeness that no one would be very much impressed. On the contrary, he stated his opinions in the most direct, blunt, telling way.' On Gallipoli General Hamilton would remind Monash of their first meeting, sitting in the shade of a gumtree in the Australian bush.

Note: a battalion usually comprised 1000 men. A brigade contained four (later three) battalions, and three brigades formed a division

1: GALLIPOLI

War came suddenly in 1914. On 3 August, after nearly six weeks of crisis following the murder of an Austrian archduke by Serbian terrorists in Sarajevo, German armies invaded Belgium and on 4 August Britain declared war on Germany. Australia, as part of the British Empire, found itself also at war. On 10 August the Australian government offered the United Kingdom a force of 20,000 men for service overseas, to be raised from volunteers. The Australian Imperial Force (AIF) would be an entire division of infantry, to be commanded by Major-General William Throsby Bridges. Command of its three brigades was allotted as follows: the 1st (New South Wales) to Colonel H.N. Maclaurin; the 2nd (Victorian) to Colonel James McCay, an old school friend and colleague of Monash; the 3rd (Outer States) to Colonel E. Sinclair-MacLagan. Monash was appointed to succeed McCay as military censor, a backwater post of military intelligence; his first act was to warn his family not to write to anyone in Germany. To his American cousin Leo, whose sympathies were entirely German, Monash wrote: 'It may cause you and your people surprise that I should take up arms in this quarrel, but then, you must not fail to remember that I am Australian born, as are my wife and daughter, that my whole interests and sympathies are British ... And that every man who can, and is able to do so, must do the best for his country.' Monash did not formally volunteer for active service until 10 September, explaining in his letter to the authorities that he was 'virtual head of four large industrial companies' in addition to holding numerous honorary offices, but adding: 'At the same time my services are at the unreserved disposal of the Government.' In fact the war was not expected to last more than a few months, a collision of giants that would quickly be over. Monash was gratified, however, when he was offered command on 15 September of the 4th Infantry Brigade (which had been raised to absorb the surplus of volunteers), and equally pleased by Melbourne *Punch*'s pen portrait of him, a gracious if grudging acknowledgment of his character and abilities: 'He inspires respect and he also inspires affection. A rigid disciplinarian, there is nothing of the martinet about him. The gods have blessed him with a keen sense of humour, and at the same time with an honest kindliness. He is always ready to sympathise, always ready to stiffen the weak-kneed, and help along the stumblers. This city is full of men who are proud to regard themselves as friends of John Monash.'

The first transports carrying the AIF began leaving eastern coast ports for Western Australia in October 1914 and had reached the Middle East – one of their escorts, the cruiser HMAS *Sydney* sinking the German raider *Emden* on the way – when the 4th Brigade sailed from Melbourne in their wake on 22 December 1914. A photograph shows Monash on the wharf at Port Melbourne with his wife and daughter just before departure: an unsoldier-like figure, middle-aged (he was forty-nine), tallish at 178cm (5'10") but corpulent (100 kilos, well over 15 stone). He wore an ill-fitting uniform and mushroom-like sun helmet. His family would not see him for more than four years.

It is at this point that the first of his letters to his wife begins. In this edition, which contains approximately half the text of the original edition, some letters dealing with family matters have been omitted; repetitious passages in others have been deleted along with those describing social engagements and the like. Where text from the original edition has been omitted, three dot points have been inserted to indicate the deletions. Monash's text has been supplemented by explanatory passages, some of them drawn from his book *The Australian Victories in France in 1918*; some obvious spelling mistakes have been corrected; explanatory notes added by this editor are placed within square brackets or in italics.

At Sea, December 1914

It was a beautiful send-off, a never-to-be-forgotten sight – the shore, the pier, the red ribbon, the cheering crowd, the towers and lights of the city gradually sinking back … into the night. By daylight we were through the Heads. Ever since it has been dead calm and beautifully cool and mild – a splendid ship, a splendid table, a most comfortable and roomy cabin, with steward and batman to wait on me hand and foot. Not a sign of seasickness anywhere, everybody happy and cheerful and working well, men all over the ship, and during nonworking hours in every conceivable attitude over all the decks, gangways, alleys, tops of deck-houses, boats, rigging, crows' nests. The horses are doing well, and are getting daily exercise. No other ships in sight until we reach the port of assembly, when we shall travel in two columns a mile apart, with ships 800 yards apart fore and aft. What a sight it will be. I am kept very busy as I have the management of the military side of the whole convoy on my shoulders. We are dropping into a steady daily routine.

At Sea, 25 December 1914

It took four church services today (Christmas) to get through the ship. No room to be found anywhere where more than 500 could hear the chaplain at one and the same time.

Large as the ship is, and ample of deck space, we are hard put to it to find room to do anything. When any considerable deck space is wanted for any purpose, the men have to be sent down to their troop decks. That is all right just now, but what will it be like for them in the tropics. We carry on board an authorized war correspondent, Mr C.P. Smith, a friend of mine from the *Argus*.

Our table in the saloon is made up of the three brigade staff, the war correspondent, and the ship's doctor, a very interesting, travelled man. The next table has the Master, the OC. Troops (Courtney), the Naval Transport Officer (Brewis) and the ship's adjutant. The drawing-room has been converted into an officer's smoking-room. The flagship seems to be enjoying exceptionally good health, compared with most of the other ships, from which come constant reports of sickness more or less serious, such as pneumonia, pleurisy, enteric, and even two cases of insanity. Of course every ship wants to get rid of its sick at first port of call, and I have to be very firm that the medically unfit must be carried on and take their chance, unless the case is very critical indeed. It would, of course, be a very serious matter to stop or divert the whole convoy. I have made a rough calculation of the cost of this convoy, and it works out at 8 pounds per minute (exclusive of pay of the 13,000 men we are carrying), so it is often a heavy responsibility to decide the best thing to do. We have been absolutely without any news of the outside world for the last twelve days, and have no idea how the war is going in Europe. We use our wireless as little as possible, and then only in cypher.

The fleet at sea is a truly magnificent and impressive sight. We left Albany in a single column over twenty miles long, the rear ships well out of sight. On rounding the Leeuwin we brought up into two columns, line ahead, two divisions in each column. Today we are cruising in three columns, line ahead, i.e. the whole convoy covers a sea area of about two miles wide by six miles long. This brings the ships to a convenient formation for visual signalling, as I have a lot of orders to promulgate today to a number of ships. Standing on the bridge of the flagship, at a height of sixty feet above the water, I can see the whole fleet spread out in regular formation, and responsive to every signal as to course, speed, distance, and interval. I feel it is something to have lived for, to have been entrusted by one's country with so magnificent a responsibility.

The discipline and promptitude in execution of orders is really very good. For instance, the *Ceramic* shipped three stokers at Albany, who had been in the *Runic*. We got a wireless to say that smallpox had broken out on the *Runic*, so I ordered the whole of the *Ceramic*'s company to be promptly vaccinated, and this was done in forty-eight hours — over 3,000 of them, including crew. In the late afternoon we have French and German classes and in the evening I usually lecture to the officers, and everybody is in bed by eleven.

The men who are not on duty are allowed to dress pretty well as they like, and the variety of design and fashions would do credit to the resources of the Rue de la Paix. We have men in bare feet and legs, men with deck shoes and no socks, men with bare feet and puttees. Some of the toffs have bought themselves white duck suits, others have their blue dungarees cut down into short knickers, with the sleeves cut out of the jackets. Others wear pyjama trousers and puttees. For top garment there are dungarees, pyjama-coats, singlets, or thick woollen shirts. For head-dress we have wide-awake hats, uniform peak caps, woollen night-caps, white caps and khaki fatigue caps. Some people's tastes run to braces, others to leather belts, some to money-belts, and a few wear the waist belt of their web equipment. Combine all the above variables into constantly varying permutations and you have a medley of garb which outvies the dress of the natives as one sees it at Colombo or Honolulu. The men are all in the best of good humour, and there is very little crime, although the 'jug' generally has a few lodgers for disobedience or answering back. For a minor offence a man gets twenty-four hours; for an aggravated case of neglect, three days; and our worst punishment so far is ten days in the cells.

At Sea, 18 January 1915

We are making for Aden, which we expect to reach about the 24th. We have, for reasons of safety, adopted a more northerly course than the usual mail route and are running on a parallel 14 degrees north latitude, in almost a straight line from Mangalore (in India) to Aden. Our visit to Colombo has come and gone, and while I was glad to get ashore, I was still more glad to get away, because the two-and-a-half days in port were full of hard work and trouble.

The naval management of the fleet is well nigh perfect. All the large ships carry a naval officer as well as the Master, and four ships are armed with two guns each and naval ratings to man them. In addition we have the submarine, which is travelling in full fighting trim, with her torpedoes ready for instant action. So now the secret may be let out that we have no independent 'escort' at all, as the fleet is quite sufficiently well armed to put up a splendid fight in the event of attack. In fact, so far as we can learn, all British, French, and Japanese warships have been withdrawn from these waters since the *Emden* was disposed of. Each night Brewis and I go into the position carefully, in the light of the latest naval intelligence received, and decide on the dispositions of the fleet for the next day, and the point of rendezvous, in the event of the unarmed ships having to scatter through an alarm of enemies real or false ...

We reached Colombo at early morning on 13 January, and I had had scarcely time to shave and dress and get a cup of tea, when an officer arrived from the shore with important dispatches from both west and east, and to arrange for the official visits during the day. At half-past nine, Brigadier-General Malcolm, commanding the forces in Ceylon, came on board the flagship, and was received with a guard, and spent an hour in my sitting-room chatting, and talking war and shop ...

During the 13th I had no difficulty in keeping everybody in check, chiefly because they did not know the ropes, and were rather uncertain when the fleet would sail, a secret which Brewis and I kept to ourselves. But on the morning of the 14th the fun began. Through a misunderstanding, the Ceylon water-police relaxed vigilance on that day, and crowds of native boats put off to the fleet, and very soon men from all the ships began to get over the side, down ropes, through portholes and hatches, and some even dived off the decks. In a very little while there were some 500 men afloat in boats making helter-skelter for the shore. Luckily a fast launch was alongside the *Ulysses*, and I did not take long to put on board an armed party of three officers and fifty men, who made for the pier and took charge of these interesting proceedings; not, however, before fully 200 men had succeeded in landing, bent on a spree. The rest were arrested in batches and returned to their ships, very crestfallen.

The escapees spread all over the town, in every sort of costume, or want of costume, each group surrounded by an admiring crowd of Sinhalese who did all they could to help the soldiers to scatter. And scatter they did. Most of them got away to the native quarters, but a number took possession of the G.O.H. and Galle Face bars, and all were very soon happily drunk. I got a detachment of white soldiers from the fort and a few native police, and then the cleaning-up process began. The men were apprehended in twos and threes and ferried back to their ships and put in the 'clink', and the game went on till nightfall. Finally, by daybreak next morning, we got the last of them on board, now sober and hungry, a sorry, dirty, bruised, and battered crowd. So far as I can gather, there were about twenty deserters all told, which is a very small total out of over 13,000 troops. The bulk of the trouble was from two ships, the *Themistocles* and the *Berrima*, both carrying reinforcements comparatively young and untrained.

In Colombo harbour we had two deaths from pneumonia on the *Themistocles*, but I decided in favour of a burial at sea so that ship was sent ahead a few hours, and rejoined us later.

Suez Canal, 29 January 1915

Of all days this one has been one of sustained excitement. It can best be called 'A revelation of Empire'. At nine o'clock the signal was made to enter the Canal at Suez, *Ulysses* leading, the remainder of the convoy following in three divisions of six ships each, at 400 yards distance between ships. The southern entrance to the Canal was guarded by a huge British cruiser, and as our flagship came alongside, all troops were assembled, called to attention, and the buglers sounded the salute, and the flags were dipped. The cruiser was fully manned, and as we passed, the bluejackets burst into cheer after cheer, heartily responded to by our men. This was the keynote of the day's experiences. We took the whole day to get as far as Ismailia – the town which is half-way through the Canal – and have anchored for the night in the lake at this point. It is a bright moonlight night, and although all the ships are darkened it is a beautiful scene, and it is difficult to realize that we are in the midst of war, and that a considerable Turkish and Arab army is within a few miles of us, led by German officers.

It took from nine to five to steam the forty-five miles from Suez to this point, but there was not one moment throughout those eight hours, and not one yard throughout those forty-five miles, that our fleet was not under a continuous storm of cheers from both shores. For you must try to realize that the whole Canal is fully armed to the teeth and is strongly held by the sea and land forces of Britain and France. As far as the eye can see on both banks, there is the most astonishing medley of military activity, and such a wonderful moving panorama of war in full being surely was never before presented to view. Both banks are fully entrenched and held by infantry, and every half-mile or so is a huge redoubt or field fortification, bristling with rifles, guns, and machine-guns. On the western (Cairo) side, every few miles there is a huge camp tucked away in the palms, with long convoys of packs, animals, and wagons travelling with supplies in every direction. On the eastern or Arabian side beyond the trenches, are miles of wire entanglements, and beyond these again you can see the patrols, horse, camel and foot, spreading out across the desert towards the outer line of observation and resistance established probably four or five miles from the Canal.

The first section was held by Gurkhas, several battalions of them spreading along the first few miles, the men coming down to the water's edge and cheering as we passed. Presently on the southern bank the colour changed to white; 'Who are you?' The reply came in semaphore, 'N.Z. N.Z. N.Z.,' to which we yelled 'Kia Ora. Where are the Australians?' 'Up at Ismailia and Kantara'. Then there was a rush to the other side, where here were again English troops, but in an unfamiliar uniform. Then there was a great cheer from the western bank, and, rushing over, we were welcomed by mile after mile of Sikhs, infantry, cavalry, Bengal Lancers.

At the entrance of the Little Bitter Lake stood a warship. The men were again mustered, and the bands brought to the deck in readiness. The warship raised the French flag and the band burst out into the 'Marsellaise'. The excitement on the warship was indescribable, the ship's company yelled and danced with delight. Round after round of cheers ('Heep, Heep, Hooray') followed us on our way, and before the ship was lost to sight round a bend, we found ourselves again steaming between company after company of Sepoys, then more Gurkhas, some more New Zealanders, an Egyptian camel corps (with hundreds of camels picketed out in the camp lines), then a battalion of King's Own Scottish Borderers, and lots more Territorials and Indian and Egyptian soldiers. The first Australian we struck was just before reaching the lake at Ismailia. He was in a tug boat with an Egyptian crew, making for a point where a number of soldiers were busy building a pontoon bridge. When asked who he was – 'No. 2 Company Field Engineers, Australian Imperial Forces.' Our ship was so busy asking questions that before our sapper friend could reply his launch had dropped out of earshot. Shortly afterwards orders came from the Admiral at Port Said to drop anchor in front of Ismailia, and proceed no farther until the situation ahead had cleared up.

So the sun set at five-thirty, and the dark came down, and the bivouac fires blinked up on all sides far across the desert giving even a better idea than in the broad daylight of the immense organization which has been launched to save this international highway.

Suez Canal, 30 January 1915

Left Ismailia at eight-thirty this morning, and continued our exciting experience of yesterday. At eleven o'clock we reached Kantara, where yesterday there was fighting, and here the troops are thicker than ever. On the Arabian side there was a huge entrenched camp of Gurkhas, Sikhs, and several British batteries, Surrey Territorials and some Western Australian Engineers.

The desert beyond is alive with marching columns, advanced guards, camel convoys, mule parks, and baggage and water-wagons. They called to us that the Turks were five miles away and everybody expects a big fight to-morrow. Beyond Kantara, we came along to a straight stretch of the Canal in which lay the *Swiftsure*, the flagship of the Vice-Admiral. Our ship saluted, and the Admiral turned out a guard of marines on the quarter-deck, who gave us a general salute accompanied by a bugle salute, as I stood with my staff on the navigating bridge. It was a thrilling moment. As we passed the *Swiftsure* a biplane rose from her deck and escorted the *Ulysses* for several miles along the Canal, circling around us overhead.

After the arrival in Egypt Monash was informed that his 4th Brigade would be joined by the other unattached brigades — the New Zealand Infantry Brigade, the New Zealand Mounted Rifles, plus Colonel Harry Chauvel's 1st Australian Light Horse — in a composite New Zealand and Australian Division, under the command of Major-General Alexander Godley, the Irishman who also commanded the New Zealand Expeditionary Force. Monash would later describe Godley as selfish, 'with a violent temper' and 'cordially hated by all New Zealanders' — which was nothing but the truth — but acknowledged that he always treated him squarely. The 1st Australian Division and the New Zealand forces, with the addition of smaller units, formed the Australian and New Zealand Army Corps — known even then as 'ANZAC' — under the command of Lieutenant-General Sir William Birdwood, a 50-year-old English officer with a slight stutter who had seen much service in India. Like Monash, Birdwood had the gift of talking to men at their own level and inspiring affection.

Egypt, 2 February 1915

Safely settled in camp five miles out of the capital, nowhere near the rest of the Australians. First night in the capital I dined with the corps commander (Lt-Gen. Sir W. Birdwood), a fine, dapper little chap, with whom I am sure I shall get on very well. The divisional commander is Major-General Sir Alexander Godley, whom I had met before in Melbourne. The weather is quite cold today, but yesterday there was a violent sand-storm and it was very uncomfortable. No chance of moving from here for a month at the very least. The Canal Campaign seems to have fizzled out for the present.

Shepheard's Hotel, Cairo, 13 February 1915

As I am to dine with General Birdwood to-night, I came into town a little earlier so as to have a chance of a quiet half-hour to write a letter, freed from the dust and constant noise and interruption at camp. One of the first of the many thoughtful things that General Godley has done was to place one of the divisional headquarters motor cars at my exclusive disposal, and it has been a perfect godsend where everything is so scattered. The car is in use from early morning till late at night either by myself or McGlynn [*sic*] or Jess or Seelenmeyer. I have had great good luck with Birdwood, and every time that he has come into personal contact with me, it has so happened that he has found something going on which has met with his entire approval. He appeals to me most thoroughly, and I think the Australian Army Corps is most fortunate that Kitchener chose Birdwood as their corps commander. Sir Alexander Godley is a man of a very different type, tall, elegant, graceful, genial and expansive – he also shows great ability. His strength lies rather in his magnetic and stimulating personality than in high technical ability, but he has a knack of carrying everybody with him ...

Of course we are still at some disadvantage, as we are not yet able to use our horses. It will be another week before we can safely put saddle or harness on them, but meanwhile I am borrowing a few horses from Colonel Chauvel's Mounted Brigade. He is camped alongside of me. [The future General Sir Harry Chauvel, a Queenslander and a regular officer born in the same year as Monash, later commanded the Anzac Mounted Division and led the Desert Mounted Corps in the Middle East in 1917-18, achieving great renown.]

There is a Territorial division camped not very far from us, and it is amusing and instructive to contrast the type and physique of our splendid Australians and New Zealanders with the little dumpy, smooth-faced Yorkshire and Lancashire youths, who speak in an almost foreign dialect and are a wonder and a puzzle to our Australians.

Heliopolis, Egypt, 4 March 1915
Rumours of our future are getting rife, but I don't believe anyone really knows. It is said that General

Birdwood left Egypt yesterday for an unknown destination. The only sure thing is that Maclagan's brigade (the 3rd Australian) left Egypt last Sunday and the brigadier showed me his orders, which were sealed and marked 'To be opened at sea'. No one knows what this means. Opinions fluctuate between Marseilles, England, Havre, Constantinople, Mitylene, and Syria, so you can take your choice.

The entry of Turkey into the war on Germany's side on 30 October 1914 had changed the destination of the ANZAC force from France to the Mediterranean. In January 1915 the War Council in London discussed the possibility of forcing the Dardanelles with a fleet, which could bombard the forts along the way into submission and then seize Constantinople. This bold act would hopefully break the war's deadlock, remove Turkey from the war, relieve pressure on Russia's southern armies, and gain the Allies a foothold in the Balkans. Winston Churchill, the First Lord of the Admiralty, was an ardent advocate of the naval plan and on 20 February Lord Kitchener, Secretary of State for War, grudgingly gave his assent that a force in Egypt, including the ANZACs, be organised 'to assist Navy' and occupy captured forts. On 5 March he ordered the first reinforcements to Egypt — the Royal Naval Division — and five days later assented to the inclusion in the invasion army of a division, the 29th, of his treasured British Regular troops. France also promised an army to participate in the invasion of Turkey.

Heliopolis, 13 March 1915

I have less time than ever for writing, as everything has

been, and still is, in a state of turmoil, field-training, organization, equipment, horses, wagons, new issues of clothing and boots, musketry training, conferences, manoeuvres, and office routine being all mixed up and done in alternating snatches of time. Three or four days every week are spent in the field, i.e. on the desert, on manoeuvre work, either leading my own brigade, or umpiring somebody else's. We have made wonderful progress, and my brigade is now a very complete, very well trained, and very formidable fighting force.

There has been a week of dreadfully hot weather, with hot desert winds and clouds of gritty dust, but a sudden change to cold wintry weather today is very pleasant.

I wish this war were over and that we could resume our lives together on the lines of some of the happy days we have had.

Heliopolis, 16 March, 1915

Everything is working like a well-oiled machine. The brigade major is a tower of strength on the administrative side … [Major – later Major-General – J.P. McGlinn, Monash's twin in appearance, who is frequently mentioned, became a devoted friend.]

My horse Tom is a real beauty. He is my favourite. He is a gentle and well-mannered horse, very strong, and very willing, and answers to the slightest hint, both as to pace and direction, stands perfectly still when told, still enough for me to write orders in the saddle, and trots and canters at the touch of a knee … He is still a little nervous of camels.

Heliopolis, 22 March 1915

Well, our war training is finished, and we are now all standing by for orders to move. Even the senior generals do not know definitely when or where we are going. One can only judge from external signs, and it would be quite improper of me to put in a letter things that have come to my knowledge as to arrangements that are being made. Suffice it to say that there is very little likelihood of my seeing England or France, or Belgium until the war is over.

On 18 March 1915 a combined British and French fleet attempted to force the Dardanelles but met with disaster. Three of the battleships exploded and sank and two were damaged in the minefields; heavy gunfire drove off the minesweepers, forcing the fleet to withdraw. Four days later the naval Commander-in-Chief, Admiral de Robeck, informed Generals Hamilton and Birdwood that the army would have to seize the Gallipoli Peninsula guarding the southern and western approaches to the Dardanelles and neutralise the defences there before the fleet again attempted to force a passage to Constantinople. The landings were initially planned to begin on 14 April, barely three weeks hence, and in an air of haste, secrecy and confusion the planning began. The Turks were not regarded as a formidable enemy and the Allied high command envisaged the Gallipoli Peninsula being secured in a couple of weeks for a maximum of 5,000 casualties. Unknown to them, the Turks' newly appointed commander, the German General Liman von Sanders, suspected that Gallipoli was the Allied objective and garrisoned the peninsula with nearly 40,000 troops, most of them close to the Anzac landing zone near Gaba Tepe.

Heliopolis, 30 March 1915

Still in Egypt, and still the daily rumour that we are going somewhere else 'next week'. It really looks as if it were getting nearer, for yesterday we had another review, this time by Ian Hamilton, who left immediately after its conclusion to meet a British division at Alexandria. The French, under d'Amade, are already there, and the harbour, and also Suez, are crammed full of shipping. So it looks as if soon there will be something doing.

What has become of Maclagan's [3rd] brigade is a mystery. Some think it has gone to England, others think it is still cruising about the Mediterranean. It left us nearly a month ago, and we thought we should follow in a week or so. The fact is, the position is only now developing and it looks as if Kitchener is going to give everybody a surprise in strategy. However, here we are still and all very well. Of course, we are losing men by death from ordinary causes at the rate of one or two a week, but I have now had reinforcements to the extent of nearly 2,000 men, so that my immediate command stands at well over 6,000. Russell, one of the New Zealand brigadiers, has just been made a general, and Godley hinted to me today that possibly other brigadiers may shortly meet a similar fate. [Monash and other Australian brigade commanders were still holding the rank of colonel. This was a decision of the Australian government, which seemed unsure of the worth of their men and their commanders. Their promotion to brigadier-general was approved many months later.]

When I rode up alongside of Ian Hamilton yesterday during the March Past, he cocked his head on one

side, in the funny little way he has and said: 'Well
Monash, when we sat under a gum-tree together twelve
months ago, we didn't think, either of us, we should
meet again so soon.' What a tremendous responsibility
that man must have on his shoulders, as it looks as if he
is going to command the operations of all the Allies at
this end of the show.

The weather is getting decidedly warmer, so we are
trying to escape the worst of it by waking at 4.30 a.m.,
getting out on the march by six, and finishing the day's
work by one or two o'clock. The evenings are, however,
beautifully cool. That the work and the weather are,
however, agreeing with me is evidenced by the fact that
Beeston, who constantly takes a lively interest in my
welfare, declares that I look ten years younger than I did
at Broadmeadows, and look in the pink of condition ...

Heliopolis, 8 April 1915

We got the first order issued today by 'General Sir
I.S.M. Hamilton, G.C.B., D.S.O., A.D.C., Commanding
the Mediterranean Expeditionary Force'. This is indeed
an historic document, but its contents are too confiden-
tial to send along a copy. A wonderful compliment to
Australia and New Zealand to be included in this great
Expedition, which I feel pretty sure will exercise a decisive influence upon the whole war.

Cairo is full of French officers in gorgeous uniforms of scarlet, green, and blue. General d'Amade's
division is waiting at a near sea-port for us to come
along, and a British division and a marine division are
also hovering about. But for real gay colour commend

me to the 'Gyppy' Army. The Sultan drives in an open landau generally dressed in plain frock suit, but wearing the usual red fez. His escort always consists of a squadron of Egyptian hussars in bright ultramarine blue uniform with silver facings and braid, and red fez. They are very smart and finely mounted. Behind usually comes the Sultana and her ladies – all closely veiled – in a smart limousine, also with mounted escort. I often pass the Sultan on the Cairo road; he visits his mother (who is ill) in Heliopolis.

Lieutenant-General Sir W. Birdwood and all his staff leave Cairo to-night. None of the Light Horse Brigade are going yet. We infantry will first have to make good a landing, and their turn will doubtless come later. Bridges is still in town, but will soon go, ditto Godley. In another week I expect we shall all be pretty sea-sick and catching colds.

Heliopolis, 11 April 1915. 7.30 p.m.

I am writing this in the mess-room, which is the last thing left standing in the camp. The car is waiting outside to take me to Helmieh station. From the moment we step on the train, all letters of every kind will be held up for an indefinite time to come.

The last of the brigade has just moved out of camp amid a scene of indescribable enthusiasm, in the dark, to the light of the bonfires which are burning up the last of our rubbish. Thousands of Territorials and Australians and New Zealand light horsemen, many weeping with regret at not being allowed to come, gathered around to give us a royal send-off. The men are in the highest spirits. I am sure we shall do well. Good-bye and good luck till I can write again. Whatever happens, my fondest love.

At Sea, 13 April 1915

We are racing across the Mediterranean making straight for the Aegean Archipelago in one of the ships which brought my 3rd Reinforcements from Australia. It took six trains to take my brigade, as you will see from the railway timetable which I sent you. All left at night, partly for secrecy and partly to avoid congestion on the railway.

The last days at Aerodrome Camp were busy ones, including final overhaul of kits, seeing that every man had all he needed and nothing more, serving out emergency rations, examining the horses' shoes, and the wheels and poles of the vehicles, and the harness and saddlery and the rifles, sharpening the last of the bayonets and swords, trying the revolvers, loading forage and stores. My staff is a formidable one, comprising McGlinn as brigade-major, Jess as staff captain, Eastwood as extra staff captain, Locke as A.D.C., and Captain Rose (New Zealand Staff Corps) as staff officer for my machine-guns. The brigade is in fine fettle. All the C.O.s and officers are keyed up to the highest pitch, and as for the troops, they are simply magnificent. The entraining, detraining, and embarkation were carried out in perfect silence, without the slightest confusion, in black darkness. We reached Alexandria at 4.15 a.m. Everybody from my train was aboard ship by 5 a.m., and by sunrise every wagon and horse was loaded and the hatches closed down.

The same quietness prevailed on all the ships. We lay alongside the quais all day, but I allowed no one on shore. After dark we slipped out quietly one by one at two-hour intervals. For the past three weeks a troop-ship has left Alexandria every two hours, i.e. twelve ships a day, all making for the same place. It conveys very little to say that the port of Alexandria was 'full of ship-ping'. It is hard to convey what it really means. There are literally hundreds of large steamers, warships, trans-ports, troopships, colliers, store-ships, hospital-ships, water-ships, supply-ships, repair-ships, depot-ships, Egyptian, French, British, Australian, and even two of the U.S.A. squadron which visited Australia.

The town is full of soldiers still, although over 200 ships have already left, and it will no doubt be another week or so before the whole of the Mediter-ranean Expeditionary Force has left. Only after we cleared the harbour, and had dropped the pilot did we open our sealed orders and the maps which had been issued to us. Of course I was in the secret, but then for the first time did the officers and troops learn that our immediate destination is the Island of Lemnos, under the cover of which the whole Armada will concentrate, with a view ultimately to a forced landing on the Gallipoli Peninsula, and an invasion of Turkish territory. How soon this operation will take place, no one can yet say. But so far as the 4th Brigade is con-cerned, we are all ready, and every man is carrying two days' food and water and 200 rounds of ammunition. Some time to-morrow we shall be in the Aegean Sea, amid the islands famed in Grecian story.

At Sea, 14 April 1915

As the day broke we ran into beautiful calm, sunny weather, having reached the blue Aegean Sea ... As the morning mists lifted we found ourselves abreast of the island of Karpathos on our west, with the peaks of the Island of Rhodes just dimly showing on the horizon to the east. It seems strange to be cruising along in this beautiful sea and mild fragrant air, and yet to know that so near to us is the centre of an epoch-making clash of arms.

After all, is it not strange that we should be fighting the Turks and not the Germans? It makes a considerable difference to many from different points of view that this should be so. One probable result of the war will be the freeing of Jerusalem and Palestine from the Turkish yoke.

Lemnos, 15 April 1915

The day broke dull and cloudy, but by eleven o'clock the mist gradually dispersed and a bright, genial eastern sun bathed the Aegean Sea in gladness. Presently the dim outline of the Island of Lemnos opened to view to the north, and on the horizon smoke from an argosy of steamers all making for the rendezvous. Suddenly, out to the west, through a rift in the clouds there burst into view the summit of a mighty mountain, tipped with sparkling gold as the sunlight bathed its snow-clad peaks. It is Olympus, the home of the gods of ancient Greece.

Arrived at Lemnos harbour [the port of Mudros] at
one o'clock. Although not much more than half the
Expedition has yet reached the rendezvous, there is a
vast collection of shipping already here. A little torpedo-boat met us about five miles out, made the signal,
'Follow me', then quietly led us to our place where we
have dropped anchor. Not a soul has been near us, and
it is now simply a case of sitting still and waiting for
orders – it may be for days.

All the afternoon we feasted our eyes on sights of
absorbing interest. A flotilla of four submarines ran out
of the harbour and engaged in manoeuvres. The airship
which we saw earlier in the day was really a huge cap-
tive balloon, about half the length of the big ship that
was carrying her. During the afternoon she made three
ascents, carrying a car containing three officers, and she
practised signalling to the submarines. Later came orders
for us to come into the inner harbour and tie up. We
went in at dead slow speed and passed close to a large
number of interesting ships, including the famous
British dreadnoughts, the *Queen Elizabeth* and *Agamem-
non*, the cruiser *Bacchante*, the French battleship
Jaureguibbery, and the famous Russian cruiser *Askold*
(which had such a hard fight in the Japanese war). The
Russian Commander waved his cap as we passed, and I
waved back. There are torpedo-boats by the dozen
flying about at thirty knots an hour; and great colliers
coughing up black clouds of coal into the hungry warships. One British cruiser has lost a mast and has a great
hole in the after funnel.

The shore is alive with troops, marching and

drilling. One division (the 29th, I think) is practising landing operations on the northern shores. No one in the harbour has any news, we are completely cut off from all the world, in this lonely corner of the earth, and no one knows whether we shall be here a day or a week or a month. We carry thirty days' supplies.

Lemnos, 19 April 1915

I was given charge today of a test disembarkation of the two infantry brigades composing the New Zealand and Australian Division, together with divisional artillery and engineers. It was a long, heavy day, from 6 a.m. To 8 p.m., but everything passed off most successfully, except that the supply of tugs, life-boats and horse-boats was quite inadequate to do the operation smartly. In the real thing, of course, ample transport will be available.

Every man landed with 200 rounds of ammunition, three days' food, three sticks of fire-wood, and as much water as he could carry. Lieutenant-General Birdwood and Major-General Godley were both on shore, and seemed pleased with the work. The men are splendid, manageable as children, and all work of this nature goes without confusion or irritation, quietly and smoothly.

Lemnos, 23 April 1915

Late this afternoon final orders for a move have come along, and, as I write, the mighty operation has begun. For some days past several of our warships, including the *Prince George* and the *Euryalus*, have been annoying and mystifying the Turks by steaming along the Gallipoli coast, and firing at their camps and trenches. Also two or three times each day our aeroplanes and seaplanes have been paying them visits and bombing them – of course the extent of the damage done cannot yet be ascertained.

The plan of operations is roughly as follows: The Australian and New Zealand Army Corps will make a landing in the face of opposition on the west coast of the Gallipoli Peninsula, just north of Gaba Tepe, our division a little farther north. Our operations will be covered by the armoured ships *London, Prince of Wales, Bacchante, Queen, Triumph,* and *Talbot,* with the *Queen Elizabeth* (the great super-dreadnought) acting as supporting ship, the *Manika* carrying the kite balloons, and the *Ark Royal* carrying the seaplanes. The battleship *Majestic* covers our left. Simultaneously with this operation, the British Division (29th), which includes the Dublin and Munster Fusiliers and the Rifle Brigade [more correctly, the Fusilier Brigade], will make a forced landing at Cape Helles, the extreme southern point of the Gallipoli Peninsula. The French will land somewhere on the Asiatic side of the Dardanelles, and the marine division and naval brigade will land just inside the Straits, on the European side. Simultaneously, the fleet will enter the Straits, led by a squadron of trawlers to sweep up the mines, and will endeavour to force the Narrows. If they cannot do this, the role of the military is to dispose of all the Turkish Army that is south of Gaba Tepe and then to storm the forts from the land side. [Monash was incorrect in his belief that the fleet was to simultaneously attempt another passage of the

Dardanelles; the Royal Naval Division, raised by Winston Churchill, was to carry out mock landings off Bulair at the neck of the Peninsula to confuse the enemy and then join the troops at Cape Helles.]

The operation has already actually begun and the first group of four transports left the harbour about two hours ago, and soon another group will go. Our turn will come in about twenty-four hours.

All we shall have to eat and drink for the first two or three days is what we can carry on our persons. And the only ammunition we shall have is what we can carry ashore. The whole operation is the greatest feat of arms of this nature ever attempted ... and it is a tremendous compliment to Australia to choose us to carry out so important a share in the enterprise. The G.O.C. of our division ordered a final conference on the *Lutzow* at ten this morning, but the weather was rough and the *Lutzow* had pulled out overnight to the outer harbour, nearly five miles away from where the rest of the division were anchored. It was, therefore, a rough and perilous journey in the little cutter which took me there, and I was wet through with spray. The pull lasted an hour and a half.

All day long transports and warships have been leaving in twos and threes, so that the game is now properly afoot. We leave at 9 a.m. to-morrow, and will probably land about three o'clock. It is astonishing how light-hearted everybody is, whistling, singing, and cracking jokes, and indulging in all sorts of horse-play and fun. Yesterday we bought four donkeys (for £9) to carry our spare kit and spare food, and these have caused no end of fun, both bringing them aboard and on deck.

It seems a pity that I cannot write more freely, because long before this letter can possibly reach you great events which will stir the whole world and go down in history will have happened, to the eternal glory of Australia and all who have participated.

At Sea, 25 April 1915

We weighed anchor in Lemnos harbour at 9.30 a.m. And sailed out quietly into a beautiful calm sea and mild sunny weather. The ships are leaving singly at about half-hour intervals, and the sight as we steam out of the entrance is wonderful to see, the long line of steamers stretching to the distant horizon at intervals of two or three miles. We are telling the men off to boat stations, in case the ship is hit by hostile shells.

Noon – we begin to hear the first faint rumble of naval guns in action, although so far there is nothing to be seen, not even any land. As my baggage has now to be packed, I have to suspend these notes. It may be many days before I can again get at this bag and this book. My only feelings are those of the keenest expectation, the thought of world-stirring drama in which we are taking part overshadowing every other feeling.

It was three weeks before Monash found time to write again to his family. The landings on Gallipoli began at dawn on Sunday 25 April when a brigade (the 3rd) of the 1st Australian Division landed north of Gaba Tepe headland, midway up the western coast of the peninsula, under orders to secure the slopes on the left flank and strike inland to cut off the Turkish forces retreating from Cape Helles, where British troops (regulars of the 29th Division) were landing. The invasion plan fell apart on the first day. By some error in navigation, the Australians were landed nearly two kilometres north of the intended beach, at a place soon known as Anzac Cove, a small beach south of Ari Burnu headland, beneath a sloping cliff that formed the southern spur of the rugged Sari Bair range, and others were landed even further north, at the base of steep cliffs. Without hesitating they shrugged off their heavy packs, fixed bayonets and climbed to the top, driving off the few Turks present, before plunging inland into a nightmare terrain of ridges and gullies. The remaining two Australian brigades of 1st Division (the 1st and 2nd) were landed in the course of the morning, meeting increasingly vigorous counter-attacks by fresh Turkish forces. This desperate counter-offensive was led by Colonel Mustafa Kemal, who, sensing that the Anzac landings posed the major threat, had marched his 19th Division to the scene from Maidos, rallied his retreating men and stopped the Australians' advance dead.

In the late afternoon the New Zealand Brigade landed at 'Anzac', its men fed into the left of the line. Monash's brigade, held in reserve, began landing late on 25 April, its first unit, the 16th Battalion, occupying a position on the ridge line known (after its CO) as Pope's Hill. At nightfall Birdwood came ashore and found both Bridges and Godley pessimistic about the chances of holding on; he communicated to Hamilton their feelings that 'if we are to re-embark it must be at once'. Hamilton replied: 'You have got through the difficult business, now you have only to dig, dig, dig, until you are safe.' During the late afternoon and night the 13th and 15th Battalions were landed, and Monash, his headquarters and his remaining battalion, the 14th, disembarked under heavy shrapnel fire on the morning of 26 April, to find the Anzacs holding a ragged front line atop the ridges, the air thick with the sound of riflefire, their beach-head barely one kilometre deep instead of seven. At Cape Helles the British had met unexpectedly strong resistance and had also advanced only a kilometre from the beaches. Deadlock had been achieved in the first day and the front line barely moved (apart from the empty gains achieved in the great August break-out) for the remaining eight months of the campaign.

In the afternoon of 26 April Monash set out to 'collect the scattered fragments of my Brigade, which had been distributed piecemeal all over the line' and next day took the 14th Battalion into Shrapnel Valley – aptly named – the upper reach of which was soon dubbed Monash Valley. From here his men took over the left centre of the line, including the vital outposts of Pope's, Courtney's and Quinn's Posts, and Monash established a headquarters in a dugout near Courtney's, just as Kemal launched a furious attack along the length of the line. The line held. The Australians and New Zealanders were proving themselves as steadfast in defence as in attack, though it was not until 30 April that their folk at home read highly coloured newspaper accounts of the landings.

Monash's vivid first letters from Gallipoli barely mention the sad outcome of the attempt, ordered by Birdwood, to seize the 700-foot-high ridge known as 'Baby 700'. Monash, pointing out that his brigade was exhausted, objected to the plan, as did Walker of 1st Brigade, but the attack, slightly modified, went ahead on Godley's orders at nightfall 1 May. By this stage Anzac casualties totalled nearly 7,000; the attack was to claim another 2,000 killed, wounded and missing. Monash's first two battalions went forward in high spirits, singing, and took Turkish trenches, but the New Zealanders were two hours late in launching their attack because of the length of their tortuous approach march, and what was left of Monash's brigade, further unsupported after the failure of British Marines to reach them, and running out of food and ammunition, had to fall back to their original line on 2 May, having lost half their men. Monash told Charles Bean, the official Australian correspondent (and later editor, and principal author, of the official history) that it was 'a disaster' and Bean thought the tragedy had left Monash rattled, 'unstrung, as well it might', while concluding that 'he was in no way responsible'. On 8 May another tragedy resulted when McCay's 2nd Brigade, shipped to Cape Helles to reinforce the British, was ordered to advance through point-blank machine-gun fire at Krithia, losing a thousand men in the attempt.

Reinforcements arrived at Anzac on 12 May: two regiments of light horse shipped from Egypt to fight as infantry, and Godley took their commander, Harry Chauvel, up to 'the most poisonous part of the line', to confer with Monash in the latter's 'rabbit warren' of an HQ. Three days later Major-General Bridges fell to a sniper's bullet, collapsing mortally wounded into the arms of his ADC, Captain Richard Casey, the future governor-general. The newcomers found that at Anzac there was no respite from bullets or shrapnel or the unending sound of gunfire.

It is at this point, in a lull in the attacks, that Monash's letters resume. The lull was not to last, for early on 19 May the Turks made their last, desperate attempt to eliminate the Anzac bridgehead, launching their entire strength against the defenders, who were by now well dug-in, with adequate well-sited machine-guns. By nightfall nearly 10,000 Turks had

fallen, 3,000 of them killed; Anzac casualties totalled 628.
The stench from the bodies and the cries of the wounded in no
man's land was the factor leading to the Turkish request for a
short armistice, which Monash describes.

Anzac, 14 May 1915

Some of my baggage having come ashore, I have again
got access to this book, and am able to send along to you
a further set of notes.

Of the heavy fighting since landing I am unable to
tell you anything except in general terms that the
brigade has done magnificently. From the papers you
will see that our losses have been heavy, but we have
inflicted much heavier losses upon the enemy. It is so
difficult in the midst of the fighting to get a quiet
moment to write at all, that I shall have to discontinue
these regular notes until we can have a rest to refit and
re-equip in some more civilized place than these moun-
tains, in which we are existing in the most primitive
fashion, living in dugouts and trenches, and feeding on
bully-beef, biscuits, bacon, and tea. I am writing within
a hundred yards of the firing-line and the rattle of musketry, and the boom of cannon is incessant.

Anzac, 16 May 1915

Apart from many things which cannot be written about
yet, the thing above all others which stands out upper-
most in the terrible fighting which has been incessant
since our landing on 25 April is the magnificence of our
Australian troops. I have had plenty of opportunity of
comparing them with the troops of British regular units

and Territorials, and the British officers are the first to admit that for physique, dash, enterprise and sublime courage, the Australians are head and shoulders above any others.

Throughout the whole of the fighting there has never been a murmur of complaint, in spite of the hardships and privations and continuous hours and hours of toil and deafening clamour. The men are as docile and patient and obedient and manageable as children, yet they are full of the finest spirit of self-devotion. For the most perilous enterprises, whenever volunteers are called for, every man in sight offers instantly, although often it means certain death to many of them. They are always cheerful, always cracking jokes, always laughing and joking and singing, and as I move among them and ask 'Well, lads, how are you getting on?' the invariable answer is 'First rate, sir', or 'Ryebuck', or 'We're ready for another go'.

During an attack a few nights ago on a ridge in front of us (which did not succeed owing to an accident) one of the machine-gun detachments suffered badly and left the gun and equipment on the slope of the hill. I called for volunteers to rescue the gun, and a selected party went out in the dusk, under a hot fire, and after three attempts succeeded in recovering the gun and tripod and all its parts. The night before last the 15th Battalion and a squadron of the 1st Light Horse were ordered to send out an assaulting party to clear out some Turkish trenches in front of one of the posts we are holding. Sixty men went out cheerily in the face of a murderous fire and only fifteen got back after accomplishing their task.

The 14th Battalion on the day of landing were sent to seize a hill, and did so with the loss of twelve officers and two hundred men, without faltering or wavering. Among those killed was Captain Hoggart, who won my shield at Williamstown two years ago – which you presented to him. Among the seriously wounded was Gordon Hanby. He was hit through the chest while trying to drag a wounded soldier into safety.

The 16th Battalion on 1 May, at dusk, charged the 'Razor Ridge' singing 'Tipperary', and 'Australia will be there'. Personally I have come through unscathed, although several men have been hit, and some killed close beside me. General Birdwood, General Bridges, and General Trotman have all been hit while in my section of the position; and about a dozen of my headquarters personnel have been killed and wounded. I hear McCay has been hit.

In spite, however, of our heavy losses (a total of over half the brigade) the men, as I say, are cheerful, not to say jolly, and are only too eagerly awaiting the next advance. I am convinced that there are no troops in the world to equal the Australians in cool daring, courage and endurance.

The noises of the battlefield are numerous and varied, and after a little while it is quite easy to distinguish the different sounds. The bullet which passes close by (say within ten or twenty feet) has a gentle purring hum, like a low caressing whistle, long drawn out. The bullet which passes well overhead, especially if fired from a long range, has a sharp sudden crack like a whip, and really feels as if it is very close. Our own rifle-fire listened to, of course, from behind the firing-line or in it, sounds like a low rumble or growl. Our machine-guns are exactly like the rattle of a kettledrum. The enemy's rifle and machine-gun fire, on the other hand, sounds as if it were directly overhead, in a medley of sharp cracks like the explosions of packets of crackers just overhead, even though the fire is actually coming from the front, a half-mile away. The enemy's shrapnel sounds like a gust of wind in a wintry gale, swishing through the air and ending in a loud bang and a cloud of smoke, when the shell bursts. Unless one gets in the way of the actual fragments of the shell itself, the Turkish shrapnel does very little harm. Our own artillery is the noisiest of all, both the discharge of the guns and the bursting of the shells being ear-splitting, with a reverberating echo that lasts twenty or thirty seconds.

We have been amusing ourselves by trying to discover the longest period of absolute quiet. We have been fighting now continuously for twenty-two days, all day and all night, and most of us think that absolutely the longest period during which there was absolutely no sound of gun − or rifle-fire, throughout the whole of that time, was ten seconds. One man says he was able on one occasion to count fourteen, but nobody believes him. We are all of us certain that we shall no longer be able to sleep amid perfect quiet, and the only way to induce sleep will be to get someone to rattle an empty tin outside one's bedroom door.

Anzac, 20 May 1915

Lieutenant-Colonel Wanliss has come through safe and well. Semmens remained behind in Egypt, ill. His battalion is reduced to under 200 and only two officers left out of thirty-two. McCay and all his staff have been wounded — Cass, the brigade-major, rather seriously, Wanliss slightly. It will take weeks if not months to get correct lists of the killed and wounded. During the first ten days the rush of casualties was so great that many cases were embarked, without record, and many were shipped to Lemnos, Alexandria, Cairo, and Malta, without names being taken, and many wounded died at sea. It will take a long time for all data to filter back to the battalion units and for proper lists to be made up. Major-General Bridges is in a very bad way and no hopes are entertained for his recovery. My own brigade has had over 2,300 casualties, but of course, many are only slightly wounded, legs, hands, arms, and flesh wounds. My killed are at least 300. Most of the fine South Australian officers you met at my sports at Broadmeadows [army camp near Melbourne] have been killed. Snowdon and Cannan are slightly wounded, Gordon Hanby seriously. Several of my Duntroon boys are killed and several wounded. The places of most of these officers have been filled by promotion from the ranks. Sergeant Pennington, my brigade clerk, was killed within an hour of his landing.

H.Q. N.Z. & A. Division, 20 May 1915

I desire to bring under special notice, for favour of

transmission to the proper authority, the case of Private Simpson, stated to belong to C Section of the 3rd Field Ambulance. This man has been working in this valley since 26 April, in collecting the wounded, and carrying them to the dressing-stations. He had a small donkey which he used to carry all cases unable to walk.

Private Simpson and his little beast earned the admiration of everyone at the upper end of the valley. They worked all day and night throughout the whole period since landing, and the help rendered to the wounded was invaluable. Simpson knew no fear, and moved unconcernedly amid shrapnel and rifle-fire, steadily carrying out his self-imposed task day by day, and he frequently earned the applause of the personnel for his many fearless rescues of wounded men from areas subject to rifle- and shrapnel-fire.

Simpson and his donkey were yesterday killed by a shrapnel shell, and inquiry then elicited that he belonged to none of the A.M.C. units with this brigade, but had become separated from his own unit, and had carried on his perilous work on his own initiative.

John Monash,
Col.
C.O. 4th A.I. Brigade.

Anzac, 21 May 1915

Information gradually filtering in from prisoners and deserters makes it clear that at least 30,000 of the enemy have been opposed to us in the fighting of the last few days, and report says that General Liman von Sanders commanded the operations in person. The only result was that we did not give an inch of ground, while we can count at least 2,000 dead Turks in front of our positions, excluding the many wounded and sick. The brunt of this fighting has been borne by the 4th Infantry Brigade, as for over three weeks we have been holding the key of the position …

Monash witnessed the sinking of the battleship HMS Triumph by the German submarine U-21 on 25 May. The U-boat topped this success two days later when she sank the battleship HMS Majestic off the beaches of Cape Helles. In both cases the majority of the sailors were saved, but the remaining battleships were withdrawn from Gallipoli, leaving the troops ashore with a feeling of isolation. HMS Goliath had already been torpedoed with heavy loss of life. Another casualty of the naval fiasco was Winston Churchill, who left the Admiralty on 21 May.

G.H.Q., M.E.F., [Imbros, Lemnos], 27 May 1915

I cannot give you the slightest indication where this headquarters is, or even whether it is ashore or afloat, or whether it is near to or far from Anzac, but suffice it to say that the Commander-in-Chief has invited me to come over to his headquarters for a couple of days for a complete rest. At Anzac we know and hear very little of what is going on at the Helles end of the Peninsula, but as to the Anzac end of the show I do know that no brigade has had such a continuously hard time as mine. Other brigades have had their turn of a change, and many of them have been pulled out of the trenches for a few days' rest and have been put into reserve; but the 4th Brigade got into a place where it is essential they should stay without relief, because they know the country and its tactical possibilities and its dangers and pitfalls and its strong points, and it took us a week or two and the loss of many lives to learn all these points. So there is no possibility of the brigade being relieved as a whole until the time is ripe for a general move forward.

I came over here yesterday, and no words can express the kindness and consideration with which I have been received and treated by all the staff. I have been able to get a complete night's rest, with all my clothes off, and a proper bath and clean up for the first time for a month. The relaxation from the mental strain and responsibility is also very welcome.

I dined last night with Sir Ian, and he was as usual most gracious and charming and considerate. Of course he remembers Lilydale, and the Naval and Military Club, etc. In fact his recollection for names and faces is remarkable, and he plied me with questions about our doings.

The attention of the whole world seems to be especially focused upon Anzac and Helles, to a far greater degree than on Flanders or Galicia (Poland). So far as British interest is concerned, this is, no doubt, because of the curious fact, which one has to think about a little to fully to realize, that we (in the Gallipoli Peninsula) are *the only British troops in occupation of enemy territory*. Moreover, our Australian troops are, in this war, the first troops of the British Empire to set foot upon any part of the enemy's territory. I wonder whether

Australians fully understand and realize this curious fact and its significance.

Today everybody feels rather depressed. We saw the *Triumph* go down just in front of Anzac beach the day before yesterday, and this morning the first boatload of survivors from the *Majestic* has just arrived at the place where I now am.

There will be some changes in my staff. Jess is made a major, and will go to 2nd Brigade to be brigade-major to Wanliss (McCay) in place of Cass who is badly wounded. Eastwood (A.D.C. To Lord Liverpool) my other staff captain, has fallen ill and is gone for a fortnight and may not come back. So I shall have to fill vacancies for my two staff captains; I have not yet decided who they shall be. I am loath to take good men from the battalions; they have lost most of their best officers. McGlinn is a tower of strength, calm, cool, collected, and a man of sound judgement. He works late and early, and nothing is too much trouble for him.

Anzac, 30 May 1915

Now that I am back I am free to say that the time I spent with Ian Hamilton was at Imbros harbour, on the RMS *Arcadian*. I learn that I was the very first officer of the whole Mediterranean Expedition who has been honoured by a personal invitation. On my return to Anzac yesterday I learned to my pleasure that I had been 'mentioned in dispatches'. About twenty in all of my brigade (including H.Q. and the four battalions) have been so mentioned, and I dare say some of them will get decorations. They gave Bridges his K.C.B. after his death.

This morning we had another tough fight. The
position at Anzac lies in the form of a rough triangle.
Our front is divided into four sections, of which mine is
section number three at the salient or apex of the triangle; number one is held by the 3rd Brigade, number two
by the 1st, number three by the 4th, and number four by
the New Zealand Brigade. Owing to its position at the
head of Monash Valley (which is the name given to the
main valley running up the triangle) this salient is subject to constant attacks day and night. At three o'clock
this morning (we usually wake and stand to arms at
three-thirty) the Turks fired a mine just under No. 3
trenches in my central post, known as Quinn's Post, and
wrecked a group of trenches. They followed this up
with a shower of bombs, and about a hundred of them
rushed this portion of the trench. It took us two hours
to get them out with bayonet, rifle, artillery and bombs,
only seventeen were got out alive, the rest were killed,
as were also at least another hundred who counter-
attacked.

The 13th Battalion was manning the post at the
time, supported by the 15th, and both did splendidly.
Burnage was hit by a bomb and had both arms
wounded. This is the first casualty among my C.Os.
Major Quinn was killed.

Although worn out with five weeks of this trench
warfare, the men behaved like heroes. Their battle discipline is perfect. They never flinch and never hesitate.
We have got our battle procedure now thoroughly well
organized. To a stranger it would probably look like a
disturbed ant-heap with everybody running a different

way, but the thing is really a triumph of organization. There are orderlies carrying messages, staff officers with orders, lines of ammunition-carriers, water-carriers, bomb-carriers, stretcher-bearers, burial-parties, first-aid men, reserves, supports, signallers, telephonists, engineers, digging-parties, sandbag-parties, periscope-hands, pioneers, quartermaster's parties, and re-inforcing troops, running about all over the place, apparently in confusion, but yet everything works as smoothly as on a peace parade, although the air is thick with clamour and bullets and bursting shells and bombs and flares. The remarkable intelligence and initiative of the men is most helpful. Most of my officers are now men who have been promoted from the ranks for gallantry in action, and they are really fine.

Also they are humane and gentlemanly fighters. I saw a sight today which is to the eternal credit of Australian soldiers. After we had retaken the temporarily lost trenches, we found about sixteen or seventeen Turks in a sap both ends of which he held. The men might have easily killed the lot. But they waited while an interpreter was sent for, and the Turks were persuaded to surrender — all while the men's blood was up, and they had seen their mates blown to bits by these very men. But this is not all. Scarcely had these Turks been disarmed and lined up to be searched, when our boys crowded round them with water-bottles and biscuits which they devoured ravenously, and then gave them cigarettes, and all the while lines of stretcher-bearers were carrying past our dead and wounded. Gallantry can surely touch no higher pinnacle. Had they set upon these beaten men and bayoneted them to death, no one could have greatly wondered after the death and torture they had spread amongst us … It was touching too, to see the gratitude of the wretched prisoners, who wept copiously and kissed our hands. One old fellow went on his knees and made a long speech to me in Turkish, with many salaams and gestures of homage. The public of Australia will never fully understand the intense admiration which all the British sailors and soldiers have for our troops.

As I write this letter in my dugout, I am looking out on a hillside which contains the bivouac of the 14th Battalion, where the men have been living for five weeks in squalor and dirt, in rain and shine, and most of them in rags; yet they are laughing and singing and joking and indulging in chaff and horse-play until it is their turn again to-morrow to face the awful ordeal of the trenches for a forty-eight hours' relief. There is only one epithet that comes to the lips of every general who has come into our lines, and that is 'You splendid fellows'. And this good spirit of soldierly endurance feeds and grows upon itself.

In Egypt I always preached to them the doctrine that my best weapon was not the powers of discipline which I could wield, but the healthy public spirit of the men themselves, who would not allow a slacker to live among them.

At long last we are to get relief, and General Godley has just phoned me that my brigade will now be relieved by one of the newly arrived Light Horse brigades, and will go into divisional reserve, in a quiet valley, where we shall be out of reach of the eternal rain of shrapnel, and where we shall be able to get some sleep o' nights. I shall, myself, greatly welcome the break and the chance to reorganize and refit the brigade.

Reserve Gully, Anzac Cove, 7 June 1915

For the last three or four weeks our position has become quite secure, and I do not think it possible now for any force that Turks or Germans can possibly bring against us to make us shift from the ground we have won – and all this is due to the magnificent quality of our troops. It is ridiculous to talk of them, as some of the English papers appear to have done, as 'raw Colonials' or 'untrained volunteers' from whom such gallant deeds were hardly to have been expected. Why, our boys, capably led, can equal the British regulars they see hereabouts at any part of the game, whether it be in digging a trench, or in a bayonet assault, or in steadiness under fire, or in boiling the billy, or in ambulance work, or in cheerfully suffering fatigue and privations, or in marching, or personal bravery. Our wounded are most amazing; they sing, they cheer, they smoke their cigarettes, even when so badly hit as to have to be carried on a stretcher.

The surprise of this campaign to me has been the excellence of the officers and particularly of the young officers, some of them mere boys, who have shown wonderful qualities of leadership. Alas, my losses in officers have been terrible. Of the 132 which I took from Australia I have only 33 left – 99 killed, wounded and invalided (about 40 killed in action) − some of the wounded will rejoin later on. The places of most of them I have filled by the promotion of N.C.Os, and, in a few cases, of men from the ranks, for conspicuous acts of gallantry.

Did I write in any of my letters about the armistice? This took place on 24 May. It really began on 22 May by our hearing, from a trench about fifty yards in front of what is known as Courtney's Post, during a lull in the firing, cries of 'Docteur', 'Docteur', and the waving of a Red Crescent flag. I sent out Dr McGregor and Dr Loughran with an orderly carrying a Red Cross flag, and instantly from all over the place sprang up Turks out of their trenches waving white flags, white rags, and Red Crescent pennants. The doctor called back that the enemy wanted an armistice for the burying of their dead (at this time there were quite 5,000 of their dead lying in front of our trenches), so I asked for a staff officer to come forward, and a very smart young Turkish officer, smartly dressed, came up and spoke in very good French. I told him I had no power to treat, that this would have to be arranged, if at all, between the Army Corps commanders and with proper Articles of Armistice; that his commander had better send an accredited *parlementaire* under a white flag along the beach from Gaba Tepe to meet our *parlementaire* half-way, to discuss the matter.

This was at four-thirty, and I gave them ten minutes to get all their men back into their trenches or we should fire on them. That same night General Birdwood sent out a letter to General Liman von Sanders practically repeating the terms of my offer, and sure enough next day a meeting took place and drew up an agreement for an armistice from 8 a.m. To 5 p.m. on 24 May. I would take too long to describe all the details of it. Suffice it to say that the Turks observed all the rules most punctiliously, even better than we did. I will give you one instance of this. While I was up on Pope's Hill with General Godley, we noticed a Turk about 100 yards away trying to repair a loophole in a Turkish trench. We signed to a Turkish officer pointing to it, and he at once understood and ran over to the man and gave him a sound belting with a stick. He then returned to us and still in sign language, with a polite salute, expressed his regrets at the stupidity of the soldier, and then very politely intimated that he would esteem it a favour if we refrained from using our field-glasses (because of course doing so would give us an unfair advantage). The burying went on all day, and precisely at five we were all at it again hammer and tongs; and now there are several thousand more of their dead for them to bury.

The weather is very beautiful but getting very warm. The air is always cool, but it is terribly hot in the sun between twelve and three – the mornings and evenings being mild and beautiful. We are hungering for news. We have only just got details of the sinking of the *Lusitania* on 9 May, and of Italy coming in on 20 May. We got today rumour of the extensive air-raid on London, but I suppose it will be two or three weeks before we get any details.

Anzac, 8 June 1915

We are bivouacked in a steep valley, clothed with stunted but green-leafed scrub, with an outlook to the sea, and in the distance the islands of Imbros and Samothrace. My own headquarters camp is at the head of the valley and looks down upon the whole busy scene.

There is great excitement this evening. A mail from Australia has come in, the first bringing papers and letters since the news of our landing had reached Australia. This valley is now one fluttering mass of newspapers – a few of which I have had a peep at. The latest date is 9 May, and I notice that in the casualty lists published up to that date in Australia, practically only those names are given of wounded who died at sea or in hospital after leaving here. None of the names of those killed in action during 25–27 April appeared to have reached Australia up to 9 May, although so far as my brigade is concerned I have used the utmost dispatch in sending on my lists daily to Sellheim, to have them cabled without delay.

I am afraid Australia will get a terrible shock when it gets the full later lists, and I grieve very much for the anxiety you must all be feeling about me. Well, I have been one of the few lucky ones, and although men have been killed and wounded around me, I have got through unscathed. My own opinion is that the worst is now over, and that the rest of the fighting on the Gallipoli Peninsula will not be anything like so severe as what is past. The Turks have done their dash, and are now terribly frightened of us Australians. They have altogether

given up their furious attacks, and it is quite probable
that our role in the immediate future (I mean that of the
whole Army Corps) will be much more passive, until
matters develop elsewhere ...

The horrible and dangerous side of war does not
really impress itself upon one's perceptions and one very
soon gets used to a mental attitude which does not
allow that side to obtrude itself. During a battle, one's
faculties are so bound up in the business in hand that
one simply has no time to dwell on the horrors, or the
wreckage that goes on all around. Of course, we do
everything that is possible to mitigate suffering and our
stretcher-bearers and ambulance people have simply
done magnificently. As for the dead, they have made
their sacrifice and there is nothing to be done but to
bury them in our little cemetery and reverently inscribe
their names in the roll of Australia's fallen heroes. That
Australia will honour the memory of all such, we are all
well assured.

Anzac, 18 June 1915

I thought you would like a little bit of the Gallipoli
Peninsula, or of as much of it as we have so far con-
quered, so I am enclosing herewith a little twig and
flower of broom, which grows wild in great profusion
on the slopes of all the hills. Among wild flowers yellow
predominates and many have a sweet scent. In the distance, in that forbidden land a mile or two away, still in
the possession of the Turk, but some day to be trodden
by us, are patches of green fields, clothed with bright
scarlet patches of poppy. But the whole Peninsula, so far

as one can judge from the peeps we get at our observation posts, has very little flat ground or cultivation, and is a confused tangle of steep hills clothed with low green scrub like mallee.

When peace comes, and we are free to move about the country, no doubt the tourist of the future will come to inspect these parts. The Catacombs of Rome will be a baby compared to the extraordinary amount of digging and trenching and road-making and tunnelling that we have done. I suppose that some day, on some high plateau overlooking Anzac Beach, there will be a noble memorial erected by the people of Australia, to honour the memory of their fallen dead, who lie peacefully sleeping in the little cemeteries in the valleys around …

Anzac, 22 June 1915

I am the only brigadier of the whole crowd at Anzac who has not been disabled in some way − MacLaurin killed, McCay wounded in the knee, Maclagan completely knocked out with nerve strain, Chauvel has pleurisy, Hughes has ptomaine poisoning, and F. Johnston has a touch of mild enteric. So I am the only brigade commander who has kept going since the beginning, without a break. I eat very sparingly, drink only boiled water, and take plenty of exercise, so that I never feel either discomfort or fatigue. The weather is now very warm, although the nights are deliciously cool; but the flies are dreadful, and make life between eleven and four a real burden.

We manage to make ourselves fairly comfortable in

our bivouacs. My home is a hole in the side of the hill, about 6 feet by 7 feet and 4 feet deep. The sides are built up with sandbags and the roof consists of three water-proof sheets lashed together. Biscuit-boxes serve as tables, chairs, cupboards and other furniture. I have my valise to sleep on, and get a daily bath out of a canvas bucket with a sponge; and at rarer intervals a dip in the sea. We dine in the open, and our cook, now that we have an occasional issue of flour, does us quite well.

Our principal want is news and reading matter generally. All newspapers are greedily seized and passed from hand to hand, but the news they contain is generally a month or more old.

It is very interesting to read the Australian papers of the first two weeks in May and the impressions of the people. Of course, all the ideas of the Australian public are based on [Ellis] Ashmead-Bartlett's fine account, but I was sorry to see that it was greatly cut down, and some of the best parts were omitted. Now this journalist did not land at all, and what he has written related only to what he could see from the warship *London* and what he was told by the wounded. He, therefore, dilates only on the first landing under shell- and rifle-fire, the rush up the cliffs, and the gradual occupation of a defensive line. But this was only the beginning of things, and much the best work was done afterwards in gaining fresh ground, and in properly establishing ourselves and in beating off the constant fierce Turkish attacks which lasted for the first three weeks without cessation, night and day.

I dare say you have heard of the death of Rupert Brooke the poet. He was an officer in the Royal Naval

Division (Marine Light Infantry) who were associated
with me in the later fighting at Monash Valley, as you
will have seen from Brigadier-General Trotman's note
which I sent along to you. I met Brooke a few days
before he died. Should any publication of his poetic
works be made, I should like to possess a copy. His career
is reminiscent of the German poet Körner in the Wars
of Liberation. [Rupert Brooke was an officer in the
Hood Battalion of the RND, not the Marines that
served with Monash. He died of blood poisoning from
an insect bite on 23 April, before the Gallipoli invasion.]

Anzac, 27 June 1915

For the birthday greetings which I know are on the way
from you all, I send, in anticipation, my very grateful
thanks. Although I know your thoughts are with me
today, and that you will be worrying because my fiftieth
birthday will be left without celebration, yet I am sure it
will please you to know that I have by no means been
forgotten. The fact got about somehow, and General
Godley sent me a birthday cake, cooked by Lady Godley
(who is running a Convalescent Home in Alexandria).
All my CO.s lined up at my dugout at 6 a.m. To congratulate me and shake my hand, the Army Service
Corps sent me a present of tobacco and matches (a most
welcome gift; wooden matches at 1s. a small box),
Norman Young gave me a bottle of champagne, 14th
Battalion sent collective greetings and the headquarters
cook scoured around and prepared for me a specially
sumptuous four-course dinner. All day long officers
from near and far came to wish me happy returns – so

that, with the feeling that I have earned the good wishes of so many people, I have really had a very happy birth-day under the circumstances.

One of my company commanders in the 13th Bat-talion was field officer for the day, and had to go around the bivouacs to inspect the cleanliness. We are all so crowded in this steep valley that the companies and bat-talions are somewhat mixed up. He came upon a quartermaster's store and kitchen. 'Disgraceful!' quoth he. 'Never saw such a mess! Don't your platoon com-mander supervise you? What must your company commander be thinking of? Don't he come near you to see such a mess? What company do you belong to?' The terrified cook stared blankly at him. 'Can't you answer me? What company do you belong to?'

'Yours, sir', said the cook.

Anzac, 18 July 1915

There runs through all your letters a sad strain of anxi-ety and sorrow, and this in only natural, but you must try to overcome that feeling. As for myself, I have got over worrying long ago – from the moment that it was cer-tain we were going to fight – and one simply goes through one's day's work. One may get into an express train with the feeling that it might be that particular train that is going to be smashed up; but that there is no use in making the journey miserable simply because that might happen. Do please try and take the same philo-sophic view and it will be all the better for your peace of mind and good health and welfare.

I am writing this letter under some difficulties. It is

still very hot between eleven and four, and the flies are dreadful; they crawl all over every inch of exposed surface of face and hands, and I have to stop every few words; but I am hoping that in another week or two the weather will get cooler, and that this nuisance will abate. I have never experienced such fierce savage flies. They fight you for your food, and make for the eyes, nostrils, ears and mouth, but they do not bite. There are no mosquitoes or bees or wasps or March-flies, so that is a blessing.

About MacLaurin's death. It happened on 27 April. Maclagan, MacLaurin and I had been together only an hour before, discussing a plan for a rearrangement of our respective lines and limits of our sections. It appears that he and Irvine, his brigade-major, went to a place which was known to be dangerous. Lieutenant-Colonel Owen called out to 'come down', and he called down that he would when he had finished seeing what he wanted to. Almost immediately after he got a bullet through the head and was killed instantly, and a few seconds after Irvine was killed in the same way. Such unnecessary exposure not only does no possible good but seriously impairs morale. While it is true that, like everybody else, I have had many narrow escapes, such as, for example passing a spot where a few minutes after a shrapnel burst, yet I have always insisted on all my people exercising reasonable caution in not remaining stationary in spots which are obviously dangerous, and in doing their observations and reconnaissances from covered places.

We are all amused at the total lack of perspective which the Australian public have acquired, as the result

of Ashmead-Bartlett's story of the original landing, and
the fact that for a long time it was the only account
which the War Office allowed to be published. Australia
seems to think that our work began and ended with that
first rush ashore. Why, that was a mere nothing compared with what followed. During the actual landing the
casualties were very light; only two men were hit
(slightly wounded) in my boat, which carried about
sixty. It was during the next three weeks, when the Turks
had got over the surprise and shock of our first wild
rush, and came at us, with odds of five to one against us,
collecting their reserves from all over the Peninsula,
and hurling themselves upon us like fanatics, in their
mad efforts to drive us into the sea – it was then that the
real fine, brave, steady work was done by the Australians.
Not a man flinched or gave way, but stayed at his
post till dead or wounded or relieved; and it needed a lot
of nerve to keep cool enough to manage my front of
over 1,500 yards, in most difficult country, to reinforce
at the critical points, to hold the proper reserves of
men at the proper times and in the proper places, to
organize the ammunition-supply, and the food- and
water-supply, and to keep everybody cheerful and hope-
ful, and to make exhausted men do just that little bit
more that turned the scale. All that was far finer work
than the first mad rush ashore, which was all over in a
few hours, while everybody was well and strong, and
recently fed and excited. I admit it was more dramatic
and thrilled the public imagination more than the long
cold nights of watchfulness, and steady devotion to their
tasks for many days after, when the men had become

exhausted from want of sleep and rough food and dirt. But it was the later work which really told, and which has put the whole enterprise on a footing that makes its ultimate success certain. For if we had not been able to 'stick it out' against those odds the whole strategic plans of this whole campaign would have had to be changed.

All my Duntroon boys have done very well. Out of the twenty, six were killed, and all the rest except two were wounded … Lance-Corporal Jacka of the 14th will probably get the first 'Dardanelles' V.C. He entered a trench full of Turks and killed seven of them single-handed … [Albert Jacka's action occurred during the great Turkish attack of 19 May. He was awarded the Victoria Cross.]

My health has kept up remarkably. I am the only higher commander among the six brigadiers, two divisional commanders, and one corps commander, who has not had to go away for two or three weeks' spell on a hospital-ship. I certainly don't like the present heat, but that will soon pass, and I hope to feel still more vigorous and fit. We allow the men great freedom in dress. I started it and the others followed. You know what 'shorts' are? They are khaki overalls, cut down so as to finish four inches above the knee, like a Scotsman's trews. These worn with short underpants, and with boots and puttees, look really well, the leg showing from two inches below to four inches above the knee and soon getting as brown as the face and hands. I have dressed like that for some weeks, with khaki shirt and no collar or tie. Even Godley dresses the same now and all the other brigadiers also. It is a very comfortable kit, especially for climbing hills.

As to the men, well, they wear the same kit as the above, but no shirts, no puttees, and no socks, so you see here is nothing left but the boots and trews, and so they go about in the sun all day, and are already blacker in the skin than the Turks or our Hindu muleteers. Of course, the men don't fight in that kit (or want of it), but that is how I allow them to run about in their spare time, and they enjoy it immensely.

A heavy artillery battery blew into my area today — four giant guns, four limbers, four wagons and a crowd of nice new English gunners in nice new uniforms. They land such people at night from destroyers, so that brother Turk may not have any notice of the little presents we shall be giving him in a little while. They land lots of them, big and little, and they have to be hidden away in corners until we can build emplacements for them on the hills, and manhaul them up.

A couple of days ago I had the rare privilege of having a fast modern torpedo-boat destroyer placed at my disposal for the purpose of making a coastal reconnaissance in connection with certain pending operations. I took two of my C.Os with me. It was a most interesting experience, going at nearly thirty miles an hour, under enemy shell-fire, and giving them a salvo of 4-inch shells for every one of their bad shots. These destroyers are prefect greyhounds, and although they are as large as many big steamers, can be handled by one man as easily as a motor car.

I am very well satisfied both with the policy and the progress of our operations. We have dropped the

Churchill way of rushing in before we are ready, and hardly knowing what we are going to do next, in favour of the Kitchener way of making careful and complete preparations on lines which just can't go wrong. For that's what's going to happen in Gallipoli in a very little while, and what's going to happen in Flanders and Belgium later on.

Anzac, 24 July 1915

This morning Lieutenant-General Birdwood came round into my section to congratulate me personally on my promotion [to the rank of Brigadier-General]. He spoke as if he were genuinely pleased and was good enough to say that if anybody deserved the honour I did. This confirms the information in your cable of 10 July, received a few days ago, and was the first local intimation I have had. It soon got about, and congratulations flowed in from all over Anzac. My staff set to work, and by some mysterious means managed to materialize for me a pair of new shoulder badges all ready to put on when the formal announcement is made.

For the last two days we have been in a state of high expectation. Reliable secret intelligence is to hand that the Turks have assembled a new army of 100,000, and intend to make one supreme final effort to dislodge us. This is playing right into our hands, as we are more than ready for them; there is no possibility of their shifting us, as not only are our preparations complete in every particular, and we have ample guns and munitions, but also man for man we have obtained a remarkable ascendancy over them, in musketry, sharp-shooting, bomb attack, bayonet work and gunnery. If they do decide to make an independent peace, the general impression is that this Army Corps will be taken to England to reorganize. So far as I can judge, the prospects of the war are daily becoming more satisfactory.

Anzac, 30 July 1915

Last night we got a cable announcing the grant of the Victoria Cross to Lance-Corporal Jacka, of my 14th Battalion. This is the first V.C. in this brigade and this division, and I believe in the whole Army Corps. We are all very jubilant about it. Unfortunately Jacka is away ill, so we can't have a ceremony until he returns to duty.

In August 1915 the Allies launched their greatest attempt so far to break out of the confines of the Anzac bridgehead. The genesis of the offensive lay in a report late in May by an officer of the New Zealand Mounted Rifles, Major Overton, that he had made reconnaissance north from No 1 Post and No 2 Post and climbed Table Top and Rhododendron Spur leading to the towering heights of Chunuk Bair, without sighting a single Turk. Other New Zealanders reported that they had walked across the Suvla Plain, north of Anzac, without opposition. The terrain north of Anzac was apparently undefended. Birdwood reported these astonishing facts to Hamilton, who saw the possibilities of landing a new army at Suvla to link up with Anzac, while the Anzacs, reinforced by fresh troops, launched diversionary attacks on the Turkish line and seized ground, namely the heights of Chunuk Bair, which dominated the entire bridgehead.

It was a bold plan, but one doomed to failure, principally because of the difficult terrain over which the troops were expected to advance. The long summer, bringing with it dysentery, had weakened the stamina of the troops at Anzac, so reinforcements arrived there under cover of darkness early in August in the form of the 13th British Division. Two more British divisions – the 10th and 11th – were to land at Suvla Bay, seize the surrounding hills, and strike south. The British troops were 'New Army', all of them volunteers who had answered Kitchener's call, but were undertrained and lacked experienced officers. The great offensive from Anzac would begin late in the afternoon of 6 August 1915 with attacks on the Turkish position at Lone Pine; the British would land at Suvla Bay under cover of darkness that same night.

Monash's 4th Brigade was to play a vital role in the break out plan. Under the command of Major-General Cox, and reinforced with British and Indian troops, it was to form a 'Northern' or 'Left' Assaulting Force which would make its way up a scrubby valley, the Aghyl Dere, marching for four hours in pitch darkness over seven kilometres through tangled, unreconnoitred country, and then attack and secure Hill 971 after midnight, while the 'Right Covering Force' of New Zealanders took Table Top and the slopes leading to Chunuk Bair itself, which they did in stunning fashion, tripling the size of the Anzac beach-head before dawn on 7 August.

Monash's task was a tall order even for troops fresh and rested, and one wonders why 4th Brigade was selected for so arduous a role. Monash's letter describes the difficulties he encountered, which resulted in the failure of the attack, crippling losses (a thousand casualties) and even doubts about his ability to command men in crisis. Monash's criticism of the Indian brigade in his 16 August letter angered Major Allanson of 6th

Gurkha on publication of the War Letters *in 1935, but Allanson's description of Monash, who, he maintained 'seemed to have temporarily lost his head' has been widely discredited. Compounded by the inertia if not timidity of the British forces at Suvla, which seemed unable to advance inland from the beaches, and the inability of the New Zealanders to hold the heights of Chunuk Bair, the failure of the August attacks condemned the Gallipoli campaign to permanent stalemate.*

Anzac, 16 August 1915

I can form no idea at all of what account of our recent operations will have reached you, although from my point of view they have been brilliantly successful, notwithstanding that the main object, the conquest of the whole mountain range, has not yet been achieved.

I cannot, of course, give you details of our plans, nor of the troops employed. The 4th Brigade formed part of the Northern Assaulting Column, and I had associated with me the famous 29th Indian Brigade under Brigadier-General Cox, with one battalion of Sikhs and three battalions of Gurkhas. My brigade was in the lead, and at 9.30 p.m. on [6] August, concurrently with a simultaneous attack all along our front, my column swept out of Reserve Gully into black darkness for its two-mile march northward along the beach into enemy territory. It was like walking out on a stormy winter's night from a warm cosy home into a hail, thunder and lightning storm. We had not gone half a mile when the black tangle of hills between the beach road and the main mountain-range became alive with flashes of musketry, and the bursting of shrapnel and star shell, and the yells of the enemy and the cheers of our men as they swept in, to drive in the enemy from molesting the flanks of our march.

By eleven-thirty we had reached the farthermost point of the beach road, and came abreast of the northern end of the mountain range. My column had the role of a vast turning movement, to get completely around the enemy's right as it faced the sea. From this point we turned sharp into the foothills of the main range, with a tangle of gullies and low ridges covered with prickly gorse. It was a black gloomy night and one could not see ten yards ahead.

The 13th Battalion was advanced guard and had scarcely entered the defile of the valley of the Aghyl Dere when the head of the column was met with volleys of fire from the ridges. My orders to the troops were to march with empty magazines, and fight with the bayonet only. Our boys rushed the ridges and drove out the enemy from them. The great difficulty was to keep the right direction in the dark. I had a guide from the New Zealand Rifles, and two Greek farmers who were supposed to know the country, but Major Overton, the guide, was killed almost at the beginning. There was a check, a momentary confusion and a few tense minutes when anything might have happened. I had to go forward personally to the head of the column to push things along, and put vigour into the advance. By dint of yelling and swearing I got the head of the column going on, and soon, as company after company deployed and dashed forward, I had the whole brigade going in fine style, and they swept forward in a magnificent dash of two miles, on a front of fully a mile, carrying everything before them, and just as day broke we established ourselves on a line of ridges overlooking the valley of Asma Dere. As the light became brighter the sight of the battlefields was one to remember. Our own losses were abut 300, of which the 15th Battalion bore the brunt, but I counted fully 500 Turkish dead and wounded and we made over 600 prisoners, including many officers, stores, rifle and gun ammunition, immense quantities of equipment, several fine chargers, telephone equipment, and camp equipment. The Indian Brigade came up on our right, but did not do nearly so well. When they lose their officers, as they did heavily that morning, the men are rather helpless, although they are fine soldierly fellows.

We dug hard all day Saturday, and Sunday was another sleepless night, during which I was ordered (much against my advice) to make another sortie to ascertain the enemy's strength on the opposite ridge. In this operation I lost nearly 1,000, mostly very lightly wounded, but the operation proved very useful in further dislocating the enemy and delaying his counter-attack. When he did counter-attack late on Sunday afternoon we were already well established and we beat them off easily, killing hundreds of them. For the next few days all hands were busy cleaning up, evacuating wounded, burying dead, collecting scattered equipment and munitions, digging wells, establishing reserves of tools, bombs, arms, sandbags, periscopes, and barbed wire and generally getting things shipshape. At last, after a week of very hard work, things have settled down, and although the enemy trenches are within 300 to 400 yards of us, we are in a strong and impregnable position. I am more than satisfied with the work of the brigade, although the men are beginning to lose condition physically, and the reinforcements are not up to the same high standard as to physique and training as the original brigade. I think that now I have scarcely 600 left of the men who marched through the city of Melbourne on 18 December last, and a ragged, dirty, bearded crew they are ...

None of the 5th, 6th and 7th Brigades [i.e. 2nd Division] are here yet, but rumour says the 5th will soon land. Bean has been hit in the leg. Schuler is doing his work for him. Young Legge, who though twice wounded, both times by a bullet clean through the neck, was both times back at work in a week. Lieutenant-Colonel Pope and Lieutenant-Colonel Cannan are still well and in splendid fighting trim, and their battalions, although badly shattered, still full of go and confidence.

Anzac, 30 August 1915

It is over ten days since I have been able to find time to write even a few lines. We have been engaged in a series of minor offensives, to consolidate and secure the ground recently won; and this meant day and night work. All our operations have been successful, but my present trouble is the health of the troops, who are really worn out after their great exertions. They are going down with minor complaints in great numbers. Where, I wonder, are the 15 per cent per month reinforcements which Australia promised us? I have had to take into my command units of other brigades (temporarily) to enable the work in hand to de done.

Anzac, 5 September 1915

Exactly a month ago we were in the midst of our final preparations for the recent offensive operations which have now been brought to a temporary close, largely through the entire exhaustion of the resources and forces on both sides. At last we have come to anchor in an entirely new part of the defensive line, a much short-ened frontage to suit my reduced numbers, and from all I can gather we are likely to stay here quite a long time …

Well, to sum up recent operations calmly and dis-passionately, I am afraid it must be admitted that Ian Hamilton's plan in its entirety has so far failed to achieve the main objective, and this has tended to overshadow the many minor successes and the brilliant achievements of the Australian troops and the New Zealanders. It is the old story – insufficient troops, inadequate muni-tions, attempting more than was possible with the means available. To assist the Australian and New Zealand Army Corps they sent three divisions of K.1 [first lot of Kitchener's volunteers] and one of Territorials and the 5th Australian Brigade (under Holmes) arrived in the middle of the operations. We also had Cox's Indian Brigade. The job was the complete conquest of the Sari Bair Range, but we succeeded only in getting a lump of it, and a fair lump too – but not all. The Turks have con-tested our advance inch by inch, and have fought with the greatest bravery and skill – but we steadily gained

ground every day. The Turkish losses have been enormous, but our losses have been heavy too – so heavy
that we can now do no more than hang on to what we
have gained and wait for reinforcements. As an index of
our losses, I marched out of Reserve Gully on 6 August
with 3,350. My parade state today is 1,037. I have left,
in the whole brigade, two lieutenant-colonels, five
majors, three captains, and twenty-two lieutenants (out
of a total of 136 officers) – of course many of these are
lightly wounded or sick, and will rejoin later.

Much of the fault with the British troops lay in the
leadership; the officers do not mix with the men as we
do, but keep aloof, and some senior officers appeared
chiefly concerned in looking after themselves and
making themselves comfortable. It only shows how hard
it is to make an army after a war has been started. I hope
Australia will learn the lesson, and England too, and that
the lesson will not prove a bitter one. But the Australians
are uniformly splendid. I suppose I have now only about
300 of those who left Melbourne with me. All the rest
are reinforcements not nearly so well trained, yet the
right spirit is there and they are so adaptable that in a
week or two they are almost as good as the old hands.

Result – although we have gained enormous new
tracts of country, our strategic or tactical objectives are
still unreached, although within easy reach with a few
brigades of fresh, good troops and plenty of gun ammunition. I am still on a very strict daily ammunition
allowance, which is rather a bother when one gets good
targets or wants proper preparation for an infantry
offensive.

Why is it that Great Britain always embarks on her military enterprises with inadequate means at first and only makes up the needed deficiencies after losses due to such inadequacy?

I am more than ever satisfied that after the destruction of the regular army in France no other troops at the Empire's disposal could have got and held a footing on Gallipoli, except the Australians and New Zealanders.

I still keep in the very best of health, and the active life has made me feel fit and hard and strong, and I never seem to tire; also my spirits keep up, although, as I lose good officers, the work of keeping up efficiency gets harder and harder. I cannot tell you how much all your full and interesting letters cheer me up.

Sarpi, Mudros West, Lemnos, 20 September 1915

Since last writing the declining health of the troops became daily more acute, and so at last the higher command, from sheer force of circumstances, was compelled to consent to a withdrawal of five of the brigades which have done the lion's share of the fighting up to now. As a result the following brigades received orders on 13 September to pack up and proceed, as opportunity offered, to Lemnos − 1st, 2nd and 4th Australian, New Zealand Infantry Brigade, and New Zealand Mounted Rifles. We are told we may expect a month's rest 'at least', but I think it will amount to much more than that, as it will take at least a month to get over the reaction everybody is suffering from before we can hope to build up either physical fitness or numbers. The whole five brigades do not total more than 4,000 out of an original total of 18,000 ...

For the past four or five days I have not been at all well, although nothing serious. The sudden reaction, and the sudden drop in temperature, brought on an attack of my old friend lumbago and a severe attack of rather acute dysentery, which is very prevalent in this island and due to microbe. I am, however, surrounded by devoted doctors, receiving the best and most careful attention, and taking it very easy and already feel on the mend, although, of course, a little enfeebled and depressed. I am quite sure that inside a week I shall be quite right again ...

Did somebody say there was a war on somewhere? To bask in the sun here, looking out over the rolling meadows and the hills topped with windmills, the sails turning around lazily in the gentle breeze, with flocks of ridiculous little black and white sheep about the size of poodles, and caravans of picturesque Greek peasants in their national dress on lines of little donkeys – one would never dream that, close by, there are armies of men fighting and killing and maiming each other. Yet this very island has been the scene of many incidents which have led to war. The Turks have made periodical raids on the Aegean islands, carrying off all the girls over twelve and all young men for enforced military service. No wonder the Greek hates the Turk.

Sarpi Camp, 25 September 1915

I have no news to give you about the war. In this island one can see the cult of inefficiency and muddle and red-tape practised to a nicety. There are ever so many gentlemen earning their war medals on board luxurious transports, decked all over with gorget patches and arm-bands and lace, acting as deputy-assistant-acting-inspector-general-of-something-or-other.

Somebody in the House of Commons asked the other day, 'Why are the Australian troops being sacrificed in such large numbers at the Dardanelles?' It's about time somebody began to ask questions, and it's about time too that somebody asked about the treatment of Australian soldiers in Tommy hospitals, for it's the absolute dizzy limit. Nothing could be better than our Australian or New Zealand or Canadian hospitals, but as to the British hospitals, here, well, the sooner they hang somebody for gross *mis*management the better.

Sarpi Camp, 26 September 1915

At Lemnos here the watchwords for everything and everybody are 'inefficiency' and 'muddle' and red-tape run mad. I only wish I dared to write without reserve about this and many other things. Just one brief summarized precis of the whole Dardanelles situation. In March last we gave the Turks ample notice of our intention to land a military force. We almost tell them in detail the date and place. Then we land a force which is adequate *only* to secure a bare landing and hold it defensively. That was on 25 April. It took the Empire's whole resources till 15 August, i.e. over three months, to land about three or four new divisions, for the purpose of making another push; and in this interval the enemy had time to gather up and send to the Peninsula some three or four more army corps to oppose us and the 'push' succeeded only to the extent of the pushing force available, which means only to the extent of the Dominion troops available. And so now it is 'as you were', and we are faced with the wet season, and stormy seas, and increasing difficulties of supply and maintenance, and no sign and apparently no hope of further reinforcements. And the latest English papers talk of the whole undertaking as a strategical blunder, and say that the whole future effort should be concentrated on Flanders, which means that the sacrifice of nearly 15,000 magnificent Dominion troops has been useless and to no purpose! Can you wonder that we don't feel very cheerful about it all?

There are some things which don't get into dispatches. It is an undoubted fact that during the first forty-eight hours after the landing at Suvla, while there was an *open road* to the Dardanelles, and no opposition worth talking about, a whole army corps sat down on the beach, while its leaders were quarrelling about questions of seniority and precedence; and it was just this delay of forty-eight hours which enabled the Turks to bring up their last strategic reserve from Bulair and render futile the whole purpose of that landing, which was to protect the left flank of the Anzac advance. The failure to do this held up our further offensive. Cheerful, isn't it?

Sarpi Camp, 2 October 1915

It is the garden about which I should like to hear a great deal more. I should like you to take me for a visit to it, and tell me how some of my favourites are getting on, and whether any of them have succumbed to the severe drought of last autumn.

By the time this letter reaches you, you will have had your spring crop of roses. Are the standards doing well? Or are the aphis and thrips bad this spring? Then there are the front pergola creepers. If any of them show signs of lagging behind, so that some parts of the pergola are getting better covered than others, in a way to make it look lopsided, it would be well to get one or two fresh quick-growing leafy climbers planted in the bare places. With the hard cutting back that these climbers were given last spring, there ought now to be a fine crop of all kinds of flowers and roses on the front pergola. The side of the house will look much better when those side pergolas are well covered with green, and when the climbing roses along the fence trellis are well developed. Then there are the Virginia creepers. How are they doing, and the violets and lilacs? What abut the pansy borders in the front? And what borders were put in this year on the south side? I suppose the lawns are going from bad to worse. Next winter or autumn we shall have to get the lawns resown, probably. Are the cypress hedges being kept trimmed and shapely? Is the tennis pavilion now well covered? The bougainvillea should be making a flamboyant show now, also the Mary Manifold rose on the south side.

By this season you ought to get a small crop of fruit, I expect the fig- and almond-trees will yield good crops by the next season, if properly pruned. Then there are the front window boxes, and the rhododendrons, and the azaleas, and the two broom-trees, and the dahlias. I should like to hear about them all.

I have had my attention drawn to the great merits of the walnut-tree, which abounds in this island. My batman Dawson has also grown them at Olinda, and says the Melbourne climate is very suitable. It is a most picturesque, leafy, woody, ornamental tree, like a small oak, giving leaves in the autumn. It is very hardy, but its crop is not much good until it is four or five years old. Then it gets better and better, and the nuts ripen on the tree, and when quite ripe simply drop off to be gathered up. The tree has no enemies, except that possums are very fond of the nuts. Moreover, the walnut wood is in itself an acquisition, and when the tree gets big and branches have to be lopped off, all sorts of dainty articles can be made from the wood, which, as you know, polishes beautifully. So what about getting one planted, say one which is already two or three years old?

Monash was on Mudros until 10 October, when he sailed to Egypt with some of his officers for an extended rest. 'I have never felt better,' he wrote in a letter home. A week later he heard from Birdwood that he had been awarded the CB (Commander of the Order of the Bath) 'for distinguished services in the field'.

On 11 October 1915 the Dardanelles Committee convened in London recommended that the Gallipoli Peninsula be evacuated. General Hamilton, who objected that the army could suffer 50 per cent casualties in the operation, was sacked three days later and replaced by General Monro, who visited the Peninsula soon afterwards. On 2 November Monro advocated evacuation. Incensed, Lord Kitchener himself set out for Gallipoli.

Cairo, 19 October 1915

This morning a telegram from General Birdwood congratulating me on being created a Companion of the Order of the Bath, 'for distinguished service in the field'. I went today into the Mousky to try my hand at buying some silks. I am sending per Captain Crane three pieces. You'd have laughed to see me sitting on a divan in the shop, sipping Turkish coffee, and smoking a hookah, while the salesmen displayed their treasures and haggled about the prices. I don't know whether I've been had or not, and don't care, so long as you are a little pleased.

By 10 November 1915 Monash was back on Gallipoli, where he found 'everything normal and going well' and his brigade brought up to a strength of 2,000 men. He encouraged his men to carry out night patrols to capture Turks in no man's land. 'It is all very interesting and very exciting, but it is astonishing how good-humoured our men and the Turks are towards each other,' he wrote. 'The Turks are real sports, and the men in the front trenches often play off jokes with each other, such as putting up dummies to be fired at, or pretending to charge ...'

Anzac, 13 November 1915

Late last night I received a message in the following terms: 'Meet Army Corps Commander foot Mule Gully, eleven morning to-morrow, service dress, belts, leave your A.D.C. and escort at least quarter-mile from meeting place'. I guessed that such a mysterious message could mean only one thing, and my guess proved right. At the rendezvous after a four-mile tramp the other brigadiers assembled, also the divisional commanders and General Birdwood. We all gazed out to sea, and at precisely twelve o'clock a tiny picket-boat was seen, threading its way unobtrusively between the throng of lighters, barges, punts, destroyers and submarines lying in Anzac Cove, and Birdwood went along by himself to the end of the little jetty, and received a very tall officer in plain service khaki, who had with him a very small retinue comprising an A.D.C., one British and one French general and an orderly. It was the great Field-Marshal Earl Kitchener of Khartoum himself. He came on to our little group and shook hands with each of us. I happened to be the first Australian to whom he spoke, and he said: 'I have brought you all a personal message from the King. He wants me to tell you how much he admires the splendid things you have done here.'

I must not dwell on what followed, but there was a long discussion, and then he went into Monash Valley, and climbed Walker's Ridge, to have a good look for himself. What he thought about it all he did not say, but after a couple of hours on shore he slipped away into the mists of the Aegean Sea, as quietly, as unobtrusively and as secretly as he had come.

Anzac, 1 December 1915

The doctors are constantly discovering new ailments, and one that has been very prevalent here has been called 'epidemic jaundice'. It resembles the ordinary jaundice in only a few symptoms, chief among which is gastric derangement, and some tendency to getting yellow. Many of the officers and men have had it, but only a very few have had to be evacuated, i.e. sent off the Peninsula. My own attack was very slight, and I am again quite normal. I stayed in my bunk for two whole days (28th and 29th), well wrapped up, and lived on rice, arrowroot, and cornflour, and the only visible effect is a yellow tinge in the whites of the eyes, which they say will last two or three weeks. I had no temperature and the only discomfort was a feeling of nausea and a little headache. The solicitude and attention of the doctors was amusing ...

But the great event of the week has been the snow-storm. A heavy thunderstorm with a torrential rain commenced on the 27th and continued all night and next day; then the temperature suddenly fell 10 degrees, and by the evening of the 28th the rain turned to snow and it snowed all night, and by daylight on the 29th the whole country was covered in four inches to six inches of snow. A beautiful sight but bitterly cold. On top of it all the weather suddenly cleared, the wind dropped, and a heavy frost set in, so that ground and snow and water-tanks, and even our sponges and flannels, were frozen hard. Since, the weather has been fine and clear, but very cold. Of course, the cold doesn't matter a bit, it is the mud and slush and wet that is liable to affect the men, out on sentry and on patrol; and time will show whether the Australian soldier is able to add the discipline of endurance to his other virtues.

Anzac, 6 December 1915

I am holding a front of about a mile in a particularly strong and interesting position, and my headquarters is located well in the centre. Our work on the roads, communications, gun-tunnels, and bivouac-tunnels is now so far advanced that one can move about almost anywhere throughout my whole position with comparative safety. The enemy trenches are on the opposite side of a valley and are from 300 to 600 yards distant. The intervening ground is useless to either side, but in order to discourage the Turk from any annoying enterprises, I am having the country in front vigorously patrolled both by day and night …

You ask about Dawson, my batman. He is my thoroughly devoted slave, and would mother me if I would let him. A hint or suggestion of my wishes or instructions has to suffice to secure instant obedience, else how could I rule the destinies and the innumerable affairs of several thousand people, under the conditions that exist here. It is on those lines that my staff and subordinate commanders have been trained, and most of them have found out that the 'old man' or 'Brig' won't stand any nonsense, or permit of any argument.

I always tell them: 'I don't care a damn for your loyal service when you think I'm right. When I really want it most is when you think I'm *wrong*' …

Anzac, 12 December 1915

Like a thunderbolt from a clear blue sky has come the stupendous and paralysing news that, after all, the Allied War Council has decided that the best and wisest course to take is to evacuate the Peninsula, and secret orders to carry out that operation have just reached here. The secret is known so far to only a small handful of men, but there is no harm in my writing about it today, because it will be very many days before this letter can be posted, and where it will be posted I do not yet quite know.

Already we have stopped the further arrival of stores, mails, reinforcements, and munitions. It would be impossible later on to remember all the details, so I am going to write a small note in diary form, each day or at a few days' interval.

The first thing to do is to secure as great a measure of secrecy as possible. This operation of withdrawal is going to be every bit as critical and dangerous an enterprise as the first landing, and if the Turks were to get the slightest inkling of what was intended, it would mean the sacrifice of at least half our men. As it is, it will mean the sacrifice of some men, and of vast quantities of munitions and stores. At a conference of the commanders it was decided to put up the bluff that, owing to the severe winter conditions, it is intended to form a winter rest-camp at Imbros, and take the brigades and battalions there by turn. In this way we should be able in two or three stages to remove about two-thirds of the total army, leaving the remaining third to man the defences very lightly , and then finally to make a bolt for the beach, in the dead of night and into boats which will be in waiting. It is of course an absolutely critical scheme, which may come off quite successfully or may end in a frightful disaster. But orders are orders. I need not say I feel very unhappy. Being bound to secrecy, I can take none of my staff or C.Os into my confidence. I am almost frightened to contemplate the howl of rage and disappointment there will be when the men find out what is afoot, and I am wondering what Australia will think at the desertion of her 6,000 dead and her 20,000 other casualties.

Anzac, 13 December 1915

The move has already commenced. To-night the whole of 15th Battalion, and about a hundred odds and ends are being taken off in barges. I am sending with them all the invaluable brigade records and a portion of my own baggage ...

Anzac, 15 December 1915

It is curious and interesting to watch the machine unwind itself as methodically and systematically as it was originally wound up. The supply of fresh meat and bread stopped a couple of days ago, and as reserves of these are being used up, we are all going steadily back to an emergency diet of hard biscuits and bully-beef. All inward mails came to an end last week. The outward mail stopped yesterday, and all the postal organization has been disbanded. Defaulters and men undergoing field punishment were released and returned to their units yesterday, and today the whole organization of the provost marshal will be dissolved, military police withdrawn, and men will rejoin their battalions. All men on detached duty such as cooks, clerks, and telephonists, loaned to or borrowed from other units, are being released and sent back to their own commands. From today the regular daily mule-train of supplies will stop, and the organization will be disbanded; after that it will be a case of fetching and carrying by hand, as we had to do in the first two or three weeks. My field hospital is packing up and flits today; after that it is good-bye to small medical comforts which a visit of inspection to the hospital always seems to materialize. Supply of firewood stopped yesterday, and with it collective cooking, so the men's camp mess-tins are again in evidence, and each man is again preparing his food for himself. Although the move is still officially a secret, the men would be fools indeed if they have not already guessed what is in the wind. Yet if you asked them, not a man would pretend that he suspected anything, and all ranks go about their day's work as if we were to stay there till the end of the war.

Later: a further long conference is just over. The actual date of the beginning of the move is not yet settled. It may be to-morrow or not for a week or more. All depends upon the weather and upon the state of the moon. Today there was a boisterous north-east wind, and the sea has come up very rough, making it extremely difficult to load baggage. The loading and landing officers today declared that we must all be prepared for the eventuality that the remainder of our baggage may have to be abandoned. This means that we shall be able to take away only what we can carry in our hands or on our backs. At a suitable place we have established a casualty clearing-station to accommodate 1,200 patients, with a full staff of doctors, dressers and hospital gear. In case there is any heavy fighting during the final stages of the re-embarkation, all casualties will, as far as possible, be brought to this station, and left there. The medical officers and personnel in charge will, of course, have to stay too. So they have been provided with interpreters and with a dispatch addressed to the enemy commander, calling upon him to carry into effect the provisions of the Geneva Convention as regards taking over our wounded and Red Cross personnel and administering same. I have every confidence that, in such an eventuality, the Turks will play the game.

Anzac, 16 December 1915

The day passed quite uneventfully. We managed to get some baggage off today, as the wind has dropped and the sea is calmer. The total strength of Anzac has in the last four days been reduced from 45,000 to 20,000 and we shall continue to hold the lines against at least 170,000 Turks (ten divisions) until the second last day, and on the very last day we shall have only 10,000. Everything is working out, so far, most smoothly. Today for the first time, I took my staff and commanding officers into my confidence, and explained to them the outline of the general scheme, and the particular role each would have to play. The rest of the day I spent in preparing a complete draft of my final orders.

In view of the steadiness of the barometer, and the generally favourable conditions, it has now been decided to carry out the operation of re-embarkation tomorrow and Sunday. Today, therefore, we had our final divisional conference, and took mutual farewells of each other.

General Birdwood himself came over from Imbros, and specially picked my lines for a visit. He went along my whole line, and shook hands with all the officers and expressed the hope that they would come through alive.

I have already sent off about 800 of the brigade, to-morrow McGlinn goes with another 800, and on the last night I take the remaining 825. These, I have divided into three echelons or groups, the first 400, the second 255, the last of all 170 – moving respectively at 6 p.m., 10 p.m., and 2 a.m. The last 170, or the 'die-hards', have been chosen from the most gallant and capable men in the brigade. Even these will not all leave the trenches in a bunch, but a few of the most daring men, who are good athletes, will remain in the front trenches and keep up fire for another ten minutes, and then will make for the beach at best possible speed. I am myself going with the first group of the last 170, as by that time the die will be cast, and I can do no good by waiting for the last small handful. The men, while very sad at having to give up the ground which has cost Australia so dear, are all very keen, and I am quite sure that not a man in the brigade will move from his post, no matter what happens, until the exact moment arranged for him to do so …

Anzac, 18 December 1915

We have worked out a very clever device for firing off a rifle automatically, at any predetermined time after the device is started. It is done by allowing a tin to fill slowly with water until it overbalances, falls, and jerks a string which fires the rifle. I have had ten rifles fixed in this

way, which will be started by the last men to leave, and
will fire off respectively five, ten, fifteen and twenty
mintes afterwards. In this way the enemy will think we
are still in the trenches, after we have got over a mile
away.

Anzac, 18 December (midnight)

The last party of the first night has embarked safely. I
have just had a note from McGlinn, sent back by one of
my police: 'All O.K. Dined with M.L.O. Curried
chicken washed down with Burgundy, everybody feeding out of my hand.' The interpretation of this message
is that McGlinn has succeeded in getting off the last of
our personal baggage, and that all troops have so far got
away without loss.

　　This now leaves me with just what I stand up in,
and only Locke, Firth (my new signal officer), and two
signallers and two police at brigade headquarters, and
800 men holding my front of over a mile. Everything is
normal, just the usual sniping, and occasional bombs and
bursts of machine-gun fire. If we get through to-night,
I feel sure that all will be well. My bed to-night will be
a heap of old sandbags.

　　As to the 'die-hards', a list has been drawn up of the
names of each of the last 170 officers and men, showing
for each man the exact time that he has to leave the
front trenches, and exactly what he has to do – whether
to carry a machine-gun, or its tripod, or its belts, or to
throw a bomb, or to start an automatic rifle, or to light
a fuse which will blow up a gun-cotton mine, or to
complete a previously prepared barbed-wire entangle-

ment for a track which might be used by the enemy.
Every one of these 170 officers and men has been given
a card, containing all these particulars so far as they apply
to himself, and the exact route by which he is to reach
the beach. All this means organization and makes all the
difference between success and failure. I think now I had
better try to get a couple of hours' sleep, as everything
seems normal, and not more than the usual noise for this
time of night.

Anzac, 19 December 1915

8 p.m. All going swimmingly and without a hitch. By
this time the A parties of to-night will have got off, and
at this moment there are not more than 5,000 troops in
the whole of Anzac, thinly holding the front line against
170,000 of the enemy. If the Turks only knew it! This
afternoon the fleet carried out a most terrific bombardment at Helles, in order to suggest the idea that we are
contemplating an attack.

It is clear, bright moonlight, but icy cold. One of
our planes is buzzing overhead, mainly to keep any
enterprising enemy plane from trying to be curious and
see what is going on. The next hour or two will be
decisive. The B parties start at nine-thirty and then
there will be only a small handful left, but we shall
have succeeded in withdrawing the great bulk of the
Army Corps without any loss, a wonderful piece of
organization.

(Entering Mudros Harbour)
20 December 1915, 4 a.m.

The last hours on Gallipoli were tense and exciting in the extreme. About nine my last patrol came in and reported that they could plainly hear the Turks digging and putting in wire, on Hackney Wick and Green Knoll, two points at which my lines have been pushed out very close to theirs. This meant that so far they suspected nothing. The last hours passed most wearily. Every crack of a rifle, every burst of rifle-fire, every bomb explosion, might have been the beginning of a general attack all along the line. By ten o'clock our final numbers had been reduced to 170 in the brigade, 700 in the whole New Zealand and Australian Division, and about 1,500 in the whole Army Corps, spread along a front of over eight miles. This meant that if at any point along this great line the Turks had discovered the withdrawal of the garrison, and if only a few of our men had given way and allowed our lines to be penetrated, the whole of this last 1,500 would have had a very hard fight of it, and many would have left their bones on Gallipoli. As it was, the final withdrawal commenced at 1.35 a.m., when the balance of the machine-guns and the thirty men came out; at 1.45 a.m. Another sixty, and at 1.55 a.m. my last man vacated his foremost position, leaving only the automatic devices working.

All other brigades and divisions were similarly timed according to their distance from the embarking piers, of which we had four. Down dozens of little gullies leading back from the front lines came little groups of six to a dozen men, the last (in every case an officer) closing the gully with a previously prepared frame of barbed wire, or lighting a fuse which an hour later would fire a mine for the wrecking of a sap or a tunnel by which the enemy could follow; all these little columns of men kept joining up, like so many rivulets which flow into the main stream, and so at last they coalesced into four continuous lines, one from the south, two from the east, and one (that is ours) from the north. There was no check, no halting, no haste or running, just a steady, silent tramp in single file, without any lights or smoking, and every yard brought us nearer to safety. The heads of the four marching lines reached the Brighton, Anzac, Howitzer, and North beaches almost at the same instant, so well had everything been timed, and so well had all kept to the prescribed pace of three miles per hour; and then, without check, each line marched (like so many ghostly figures in the dim light) in single file on to its allotted jetty, the sound of marching feet having been deadened by laying a floor of sandbags; and so on to a motor barge ('beetles' we call them) holding 400. On to these, generals, staff officers, machine-gunners and privates all packed up, promiscuously and quietly. There was a short pause to make sure that no one had been left behind. Not a sound could be heard on the shore except the throb, throb of the beetle's engines, and on the distant hills, the spasmodic rifle-shots of the enemy, discharged at our now empty trenches.

Then the landing and loading staff, chiefly naval officers, stepped aboard. 'Let go all over – right away' was the last order, and slowly we moved out. Just before the barge at Anzac pier cast off, the last engineer officer on shore joined the terminals of an electric battery and thereby fired three enormous gun-cotton mines. These with a terrific explosion blew up 'Russell's Top', which was the knoll at the head of the western branch of Monash Valley, and which, though we could never drive the Turks off it, we had succeeded in tunnelling under. With the knoll a couple of hundred Turks must have gone up in the air, but nothing could be seen except a volcano of dust. Instantly a most terrific tornado of rifle and machine-gun fire burst forth along the whole length of Sari Bair, showing that the Turks, far from suspecting our real manoeuvre, had been actually expecting an attack of which they took the firing of the mine to be the first signal. Thus, dramatically, with the bullets, aimed at our trenches, high up on the slopes and spurs of the range, whistling harmlessly overhead, we drew off in the light of the full moon, mercifully screened by a thin mist, and so ended the story of the Anzacs on Gallipoli.

We had succeeded in withdrawing 45,000 men, also mules, guns, stores, provisions and transport valued at several million pounds, without a single casualty, and without allowing the enemy to entertain the slightest suspicion. It was a most brilliant conception, brilliantly organized, and brilliantly executed, and will, I am sure, rank as the greatest joke – and the greatest feat of arms – in the whole range of military history.

Arrived at last on the little transport *Arran*, packing closely on her two decks, in her little cabins and her little saloon, officers and men of Army and Navy foregathered, from upwards of fifty different units, men who had not seen or heard of each other since the days of the war training in Egypt, or since leaving our home lands.

The strain being over, the reaction came in wild and hilarious greetings, mutual felicitations and hearty hand-shakes all around. The steamer got under way for Lemnos, and the sights and sounds of Gallipoli dropped back into the past. Gradually the ship's company, worn out with want of sleep and the tremendous strain of the closing hours, fell asleep in all sorts of attitudes, on saloon tables, on decks, in alleyways, and on hatches. I got a bunk in the pantryman's cabin, but found myself quite unable to sleep, so decided to write down my impressions while they were still fresh. It is now 6.30 a.m. And we're just dropping anchor in the outer roadstead of Mudros Harbour, and a new day is breaking.

6 p.m. – There is little to add to the story. Brigadier-General Johnston (New Zealand Chief of our Artillery) has just landed. He went on board a destroyer to direct naval fire, in case we had been attacked. He relates that at nine o'clock this morning and again at twelve o'clock noon the Turks opened a furious bombardment on our empty trenches, particularly at Lone Pine, the Apex and Hill 60 (the last two being the ends of my portion of the line). So up till then they had not yet discovered our departure, even though our destroyers had amused themselves all the morning in shelling our beaches and hospitals (which had been left standing), with incendiary shells, so as to burn up the debris of wreckage which

we had created, and deprive the Turks of anything of possible value to them.

This is the end of the story of Gallipoli so far as the Army Corps is concerned. And now we turn our energies to gathering up our details from all over the island, to sorting out units, forming camps, refitting, and standing by for the next orders. What they may be no one knows – Helles, or Salonika, or France, or Cairo, or the Canal.

The last British troops were evacuated from Cape Helles on 8 January 1916. The Gallipoli campaign had claimed 266,000 Allied casualties of whom 46,000 were fatalities, killed in battle or dead from disease. Turkish losses are estimated to have been between 250,000 and 400,000. Turkey's military strength never recovered from these heavy losses.

II: WESTERN FRONT

Ismailia, Egypt, 15 January 1916

I am having a furiously busy time. It is very much worse than in February and March last, for I am working now with blunted tools, and instead of a newly raised, experienced, and competent body of regimental officers, I have only the remnants, most war weary. In other words, organization is a very much easier job than reorganization ...

Moascar Camp, Ismailia, 14 February 1916

Orders have now come out for the four veteran Australian brigades to each split into two, making the nucleus of four new brigades, to be called the 12th, 13th, 14th and 15th. My twin brigade will be the 12th and it will probably be commanded by Godfrey Irving, late Chief of General Staff in Australia. As it turns out, I shall lose none of my H.Q. or signals, or battalion C.Os or their H.Q. or machine-guns, but only about eight officers and five hundred men per battalion which I shall speedily make up out of reinforcements already in Egypt. The 13th Brigade will be similarly

formed out of the 3rd Brigade; and the three brigades,
i.e. the 4th, 12th and 13th, will together form the 4th
Australian Division. As to who will command this division, nothing is finally settled yet, but there are
indications that it will be Major-General Sir H.V. Cox,
the same who formally commanded the 29th Indian
Brigade, which fought with us in August and September last in the Aghyl Dere.

*Monash was angry when Cox was promoted to command the
new 4th Australian Division and described him as 'one of those
crochetty, peppery, livery old Indian officers'. He wrote to his
old friend Major-General James McCay to push his claim for
command of one of the new divisions, but without success. He
was embittered over the woefully mismanaged Gallipoli campaign and critical of British generals like Godley — 'the Army
Clique which holds all Militia officers in contempt as "mere
amateurs" '. He suspected, with some foundation, that some of
the authorities regarded his German-Jewish background with a
certain suspicion.*

Ismailia, 15 February 1916

Farewell functions between us and the New Zealanders
have already commenced. To-night the Maori Contingent gave a campfire concert and the principal number
was a 'haka' especially composed in my honour. It was
most amusing to see their doctor and chaplain, both of
whom are highly educated gentlemen, stripped and tat-
tooed in war-paint, and going through cannibalistic
antics with their men.

Serapeum, 29 March 1916

We arrived here day before yesterday, and it is quite the most horrible place of any we have yet been in. Between eleven and four it is almost unbearably hot in the sun although the nights are cool; but with the slightest breeze, the fine dust of the desert lifts and travels in clouds so dense that one cannot see for fifty yards, and the dust covers everything, food and all, with a thick layer. Intense heat, dust, and myriads of savage flies and sandflies which bite and leave water blisters all over hands and head; at least for those who have no flynets. Your green flynets are well chosen and will be no end of comfort out on the desert.

Serapeum, 8 April 1916

Our future plans are now taking more definite shape, and in view of cables which have been passing between the War Office and Murray there is every reason to expect that we shall go to France some time about the end of May. The 1st and 2nd Divisions are already in France, the New Zealand Division left last week, and the 4th and 5th are to go as soon as equipped and trained. The Mounted Division (Chauvel) will probably remain in Egypt for the present. Here, matters are very dull. The nearest Turkish post from here is sixty miles away, and next week we are sending out a Camel Patrol to try and bag the whole post. But all thoughts of a Turkish invasion of Egypt are over for this year at any rate, and perhaps the war will be over before next year. Let's hope so.

Cairo, 15 April 1916

I wanted to make a few purchases and to have a couple of days' rest and quiet so I have come to Cairo. But most of all I wanted to get away from the terrible khamsin! It occurs in lower Egypt on about thirty days in the year, but most frequently in April, May, and June. None who has experienced it is ever likely to forget it. It is, of course, much worse out in the desert than in the cities, but even in the cities it is bad enough. You have heard tell of siroccos, and tornadoes, and hurricanes, and simooms. The khamsin is the archfiend of them all. The prevailing wind in Egypt in the summer is from the north and north-west. It is cool and seldom strong enough to raise dust or be disagreeable. But when the breeze swings round to the south or south-west, beware! For any such wind may be precursor of a khamsin.

Thursday broke with a calm. By seven o'clock a strong breeze sprang up from the south-west, by nine o'clock it commenced to come in gusts of gale, raising and carrying clouds of dust. By noon, it had reached hurricane force, and seemed to lift the desert up bodily into the air. For the sun and sky were blotted completely out, and the air for a height of hundreds of feet was thick with dust and grit and sand and even pebbles of gravel. It was quite impossible to stand up in it, much less to face it. Down went one building after another — mess sheds, cookhouses, canteens. Tents not perfectly anchored were torn up from their moorings and disappeared into the black vault overhead like derelict sheets of paper. The tents and marquees that stood, rocked and strained at their guys, while the sand and pebbles rained like hail upon their weather sides. The fine dust was even forced through the fabric of the canvas and came down in copious showers upon everything in the tents. In less than no time papers, documents, bedding, clothing, food, meat in the butcheries were covered with layer upon layer of thick dust.

Outside everything was blotted out of sight; nothing more than thirty yards away was visible. Horses screamed in terror and plunged at their heel-ropes; parties of men caught out in the storm lost their bearings; several men walked head-first into moving wagons; one poor devil was run over and killed by our little steam railway which supplies the camps. Horse rugs, harness, kits, anything lying on the face of the country was changed, hills disappeared and appeared again where there had been hollows. And this went on for twenty mortal hours, the fury of it not abating for an instant. It was impossible to move about, or eat or cook or sleep. There was nothing to do but huddle together in the most secure of the tents and swear, and wonder if it was ever going to stop. But stop it did at last, and by midday Friday, although the wind was still strong and hot and stifling, the dust and sand had ceased to fly. And it left us gasping, choking, eyeballs inflamed, chests raw with coughing, with severe headaches and symptoms of catarrh in nose and throat, and generally down and out. It will take a week to repair the wreckage of buildings and works, and shovel out trenches and roads, and railways and pits and drains, all covered and filled chock-full of sand.

I shall never forget my ride from my camp three

miles east of the Canal to Serapeum No. 1 Siding, two miles west of the Canal. The five miles took three hours and it was all I could do to make Tom face it. Arrived at where the railway had once been, I found hundreds of soldiers digging away sand to find it, and it was not until they had dug out the railway that the train could come in to take us away. Then the journey (via Ismailia to Cairo) under one hundred miles, took eight hours, so that I was a sorry spectacle when I got there, and was glad to get a hot bath and go to bed without anything to eat. And I slept for eleven hours.

Serapeum, Egypt, 22 April 1916

Now, good people, don't worry about me or my advancement. For me it counts for very little. If they want me to command a division they know where to find me. So far nobody has passed over me. McCay, Chauvel and Legge are all my seniors. I might have had the 4th Division. Pearce cabled Birdwood asking that either White or I might get it; but Birdwood preferred to entrust it to Cox, a Kitchener man, and an old Indian colleague. It is rather worrying to be constantly reminded of the great advancements my friends predict for me. My thoroughly successful command of my own brigade, and my satisfactory performance of every task set my brigade is quite good enough for me, and I know what Cox, and Godley and Birdwood and Murray think of me and my brigade! Brudenell White (Brigadier-General) was Director of Operations in Australia. He was Bridges' right-hand man. He was the General Staff Officer, first grade (G.S.O.I.) of Bridges' division. Later

on he was Chief of the General Staff of Birdwood's
Army Corps. He is far and away the ablest soldier Australia has ever turned out. You will remember meeting
him at the Roosevelt reception at the Ritz. He is also a
charming good fellow.

Serapeum, 26 April 1916

I must tell you about the celebration of 'Anzac Day' yesterday. I turned out the whole brigade with all attached
units at 6.45 a.m. Every man who had served on Gallipoli wore a blue ribbon on the right breast, and every
man, who, in addition, had taken part in the historic
landing on 25 April 1915, wore a red ribbon also. I am
enclosing mine to you as a keepsake. Alas, how few of
us are left who were entitled to wear both. We then had
a short but very dignified service, ending with a fine
stirring address by Chaplain Lieutenant-Colonel Wray
(who landed with us). Then the massed bands of the
brigade played 'The Dead March in Saul' while the
parade stood to attention, then the massed buglers blew
the 'Last Post'. For the rest of the day everyone was
given a whole holiday …

Godley and his staff came down from Ismailia, and
at about five, the Prince of Wales came up in his little
pinnace from Suez where he had been spending the
day, and stayed an hour with us, heartily enjoying
the fun, and the afternoon-tea, and the ovation of cheers
the men gave him wherever he went. We sent cables to
5th Division, to Birdwood, and to 1st Anzac in France.
In the evening we had mess dinners everywhere, and
finished up with band concerts, and wished each other

the opportunity of enjoying many happy returns of this
famous day – *Our Day*.

Serapeum, 15 May 1916
The shade temperatures for the last four days have been
106 – 108 – 109 – and millions and millions of flies.
The date of our expected departure for France is drawing near. Although we have nothing definite to go
upon, we are all fervently hoping to get away from this
dreadful desert before the end of the present month.

Serapeum, 28 May 1916
We move on or about 1 June. Fourth Brigade is the first
to move. Locke goes to-morrow. I command the First
Flight comprising about 6,000 troops. My flight will
take about eight ships. Letters from 2nd Division, who
have been in France since the middle of March and have
just got into the front line go to show that the conditions are not nearly so severe as at Anzac. They say the
Western Front is a picnic to what Gallipoli was.

France, 12 June 1916
We left Serapeum on 31 May. After I had seen the bulk
of my flight on to troop trains at Serapeum sidings, I
came along with one staff officer to Alexandria by pas-
senger train, and went straight to the Quay Gabarry and
on to the transport *Transylvania* where my ship's staff
(consisting of adjutant, quartermaster, baggage master,
sergeant-major, and sergeant-clerk) had preceded me
the day before to get the embarkation ready. My ship
took 3,200, the rest of the brigade with the horses and

vehicles went on to the *Canada* and *Havreford*. By nightfall on 1 June I had everything embarked and we sailed
at daybreak on 2 June. Our voyage was quite uneventful, warm and dead calm on the way. We followed a
tortuous course to dodge the submarines, but had not a
single scare. While at sea we got wireless news of the
North Sea battle and of the loss of Earl Kitchener. [Lord
Kitchener was drowned at sea en route to advise the
Russian armies on 5 June, 1916 when the cruiser HMS
Hampshire, in which he was sailing, hit a mine in the
North Sea.]

We reached Marseilles in the early morning of
7 June and Wednesday was a busy day, unloading and
dispatching units by different trains to different destinations. I found a compartment reserved for me on the
night express *wagon-lit*, and with Durrant had a most
comfortable journey, reaching Paris at eight o'clock on
Thursday morning. As the first of my troop trains could
not possibly reach Calais before Saturday evening, I
decided to spend a day in Paris. Although there is a
sombre air over the whole city, and very large numbers
of people are in black, and the streets are full of soldiers,
yet there is a good deal of life in the streets still.
Of course the Louvre and many other galleries and
museums are closed. But we managed to put in a good
deal of sightseeing including Place de la Concorde, Arc
d'Etoile, Luxemburg gallery, les Invalides (Napoleon's
tomb), Eiffel Tower (closed), Musee Grevin, Palais Royal,
and Arc de Carousel. On Thursday evening we visited
Folies Bergère and saw a revue, but as all sale of drinks
is stopped after 9.30 p.m. the streets were deserted by

11 p.m. and night life was stopped absolutely.

We went on to Calais on Friday. On the Calais route all is under military control, so there are neither sleeping- nor dining-cars and practically only soldiers travelling. It took us all night to make the run which in peace time takes five hours. Arrived at Calais at 7.30 a.m. on Saturday, we learnt for the first time our approximate destinations; after a long wait we got a troop train going east, which after two hours, dropped us at Hazebrouck where we found a motor car sent down to met us by 1st Anzac (Birdwood). We motored to Merris, which will be our 4th Divisional Headquarters, and hence to this town which is my headquarters. Here I found Locke who had gone ahead to make preliminary arrangements, and we at once set to work to billet our brigade, on which task we have been engaged ever since. From all I can gather the part of the front allotted to Dominion troops is very quiet ...

I have allotted to me an area, called a Brigade Area, in which all the troops belonging to or associated with the brigade are billeted. This area is very extensive covering fully sixty square miles; so that it is impossible to get on without a good fast Daimler motor car which has been placed at my disposal. The shape of the area is something like a pear, the stalk end up. At this end there is the one fair-sized town of the district, about 14,000 civilian inhabitants. The remainder of the area is dotted all over with villages large and small, and farms innumerable. The whole countryside is resplendent with spring foliage, herbage, flowers and crops galore, and beautiful country lanes between blackthorn hedges run in every direction. Brooks and canals intersect the whole area, scattered about by platoons and companies ...

This town is a truly astonishing place. It is within seven kilometres of our front trenches. Our artillery is on its eastern outskirts. When our guns are not making a noise we can hear the Boche guns quite plainly. Aeroplanes, both ours and enemy's, often fly overhead (there was quite a pretty though inconclusive airfight this afternoon). Yet in spite of all this the town is in full swing and teeming with life, except that one sees nothing but women and children and old men and British and French soldiers and motor lorries and automobiles. The Hotel de Ville is an army corps headquarters (not Australian). My own 'billet' is a two-storey mansion, in a street just off the town market square. The lower storey is devoted to our offices and mess rooms and my private sitting-room, while the top storey has a separate bedroom for each of us, Locke, Durant, and Eric Simonson. Our cooks and servants occupy the attics. The town is replete with every comfort, a plenitude of fresh eggs and butter, fruit, vegetables, fresh fish, poultry, cheese, still and sparkling wines, delicatessen of all kinds; while in the shops there is nothing you can think of that you cannot buy, from Maltese or Honiton lace to a kit of carpenter's tools. And if by chance you can think of anything the shops haven't got, they'll understand and get it for you from London or Paris in forty-eight hours. I came here thinking to find a ruined devastated country, without population, with farms and fields laid waste, buildings and churches in ruins and a population of refugees living in misery. Yet here, within four and a half miles of the German Army, I find a peaceful, prosperous, medieval Flemish (once Spanish) town, full of life, and in spite of its sixteenth century church and its fifteenth century town hall and market square, replete with the most up to date civilized comforts, and a people calm, sedate, confident, and utterly unconcerned as to the terrible slaughter going on within earshot.

France, 24 June 1916

For days there have been rumours in well-informed quarters that I am to get the 3rd Division. Today I am told by a highly placed officer on an Army Corps Staff, that this rumour 'though still unofficial, is quite reliable'. He added that 'approval of this appointment has been received from Australia'.

Two days later Birdwood told Monash that he (Monash) was to take command of the new 3rd Australian Division, which was being formed in England from newly arrived Australian units. Monash's pleasure was muted by his regret at parting company with his 4th Brigade, which he had led for nearly two years, and which became part of 4th Division.

France, 9 July 1916

A few moments ago I received a letter from B. in which he tells me the name of my successor in my present office, and that he will join me to take over upon his return from leave in a day or two. He also says in the letter that orders have just been issued by the W.O. for 'your new staff to go over and take up their appointments' and that orders re myself will probably be issued 'in the course of the next few days'. We are pulling out of the line, commencing Monday, completing Tuesday.

London, 18 July 1916

The matter about which you will most want to know is – my new command and all that it means. Will it weary you if I give you a brief account of what a division is? First of all there is divisional headquarters about which I shall give more details later, and which apart from my staff comprises some eighty clerks, grooms, batmen and police, and associated with which is a squadron of cavalry (Light Horse). There is the Divisional Signal Company, which runs my telegraphs, telephones, and wireless – with four sections, one for headquarters and one for each infantry brigade.

The Artillery comprises Divisional Artillery, under brigadier-general (Grimwade) – three field and one Howitzer Artillery Brigade (each of four batteries, each of four guns), each having a Brigade Ammunition Column; also the D.A.C. (Divisional Ammunition Column).

The Engineers comprise the headquarters (under C.D.E. Commander Divisional Engineers) who has under him three Field Companies of Engineers, the Pioneer Battalion, and the Pontoon and Bridging train.

The Infantry comprises the 9th, 10th and 11th Australian Infantry Brigades, each with its Machine-Gun Company and Light Trench-Mortar Battery; each brigade under a brigadier-general (Jobson, McNicoll and Rankine). Of the twelve battalions only two are commanded by old 4th Brigade officers (Rankine and

Mansbridge). Total Infantry 13,500 ... The whole command comprises over 20,000 troops, 7,000 horses, 64 guns, 192 machine-guns, 18 motor cars, 82 motor lorries, and 1,100 other vehicles, so that you will see that it is some army ... My staff is a very fine one, carefully selected, mostly English and Indian officers ...

The division is now beginning to arrive in England, one infantry and two artillery brigades are already here, and others are due today. I take up my quarters at Salisbury Plain on Monday next, and start systematic organizing and training. It will take a minimum of six weeks but may, of course, take much longer. My own promotion to major-general is not yet announced but that is only a matter of a week or two, as it has to be done in Australia by the Federal Executive Council. I suppose McCay and I are the only citizen officers in the whole Empire to have attained this grade. My parting with the 4th Brigade was indeed a sad one, but everybody has been most kind.

Salisbury Plain, 11 August 1916

There is very little news to tell you about the division. Everything is going swimmingly and I have had no reason to abate my good opinion of the quality and prospects of the division. The units are not yet complete; the 38th arrived yesterday, and the 40th from Tasmania is still to come. McCormack arrived yesterday with No. 10 Field Company, and with messages from you and many friends.

Training is going on most smoothly and energetically, and I have had no trouble at all. There has been a revival of the rumour that Australia will not be able to keep up the necessary flow of reinforcements to feed five divisions in the field, and that it may therefore be found necessary to break up the 3rd Division and use it as reinforcements to the other four. It would be a very foolish thing to do. I merely mention it as of passing interest.

Lark Hill, 26 August 1916

The work to be done in the division is stupendous; and it will be greatly to my credit if I can get the division ready for service overseas quickly ... Two N.C.Os are McGrath and Ozanne, Federal members respectively for Ballarat and Geelong. Carmichael, Minister for Education in New South Wales, is a lieutenant in the 9th Brigade (36th Battalion). McNicoll is commanding the 10th Brigade very ably. I have recommended Cannan for the 11th Brigade, he will join me at end of August. Law commands the Pioneers, McCormack has the No.20 Field Company, which is full of University students and engineering graduates. Gunsen is senior chaplain of the division. Grimwade is divisional artillery commander. Dowse has the divisional train. Brissenden, K.C., LL.D. in New South Wales, is a corporal and is a clerk at divisional headquarters.

There are numbers of old Anzac friends such as Rankine, Simpson, Mansbridge, and Morshead.

The 3rd Division is now complete in all its details and is doing extremely well, and I am getting a lot of praise from highly placed War Office people for our splendid progress, but I am afraid it will be near the end of October before they can let me have all the rifles, guns and horses I need to equip us for service overseas. I have now got a good grip of my new job, and entertain no fear about being able to make a success of it ...

Lark Hill, 10 September 1916
I don't know whether you have heard of the glorious doings of the 4th Brigade. All the great and successful offensives north of Pozières were carried out by them. They attacked on six successive nights and succeeded brilliantly on each occasion, against the Prussian Guard, and held all ground won, and took hundreds of prisoners. General Birdwood has issued an order extolling the great successes of the 4th Brigade, and holding them up to the emulation of the rest of the Army Corps.

Durrington (near Lark Hill), 16 Septeber 1916
There is no prospect of our going to France for at least another six weeks, owing to shortage of rifles, guns and horses. They simply haven't got them in England to give us. After fitting out the Serbians and Russians, the War Office have left themselves very short of essential requirements, and the 3rd Australian and several other British divisions (new ones) will have to be held up in consequence.

It is hard to convey to you the tremendous effort the nation is making. The whole country is one huge workshop, and everywhere the manufacture of equipment, ships, torpedoes, rifles, guns, shells, aeroplanes, airships, trench-mortars, and totally new types of weapons, is going on in most amazing quantities. Guns of the largest calibre are being turned out by the hundred, field-guns by thousands, battleships by the dozen, and so on. It is only now that the effect of all this activity is beginning to be felt, and one realizes that the British Army has not yet really begun the war in earnest ...

Lark Hill, 30 September 1916

The great event of the fortnight has been the King's Review, which came along sooner than I had expected. It was for the division a veritable triumph, and, apart from being by far the biggest and most splendid, it was much the most successful review I have ever been present at. In addition to the 3rd Division I had on parade several thousand Australian and New Zealand depot troops (training battalions), and the parade was a grand total of 27,000. Had they marched in column of route, it would have taken five hours to pass a point. As it was, we marched past, in close column of platoons (i.e. 100 men every ten paces), and even with this crowding, the march took nearly two hours. The King was not due till 11.15 a.m., but the earliest units had to start for the ground at 7.15 a.m., even though we had five different roads of approach to Bulford Field where the review was held.

I suppose it does not happen to very many people to have the privilege and pleasure of spending two and a half hours continuously, and without interference or interruption by a single other person, with the King of so mighty an Empire, and talking with him the whole

time on a footing of perfect freedom, so it will doubtless interest you to have a brief record of the things we
talked about.

The King wore ordinary khaki uniform; was, in
fact, dressed exactly like myself, horse furniture, and all
else identical, except that he wore on his shoulders the
badges of a field-marshal, and below them two small
crowns with the royal ciphers 'E.R.' and 'V.R.' below
them respectively the two sovereigns under whom he
had served. He rode a beautiful black horse. His sole
personal retinue comprised two equerries – Commander Sir Charles Cust (Naval) and Major Clive Wigram
(Military) – one standard-bearer carrying a tiny Royal
Standard on a lance, and one servant in a black top-hat
and long frock-coat …

My own retinue comprised my A.D.C. (Eric
Simonson), my G.S.O.I. (Jackson), my A.A.G (Farmar),
one standard-bearer (one of my mounted military
police, a splendid Australian, 6 feet 7 inches tall), and one
mounted trumpeter …

As the King rode up to the flagstaff, the great Royal
Standard (which had been coiled up in a ball at the
mast-head) was broken. It fluttered out into the breeze
as I gave the 'Royal Salute', and 27,000 bayonets flashed
together into the 'Present Arms', and the sixteen massed
bands played six bars of the anthem. It was a moment of
glorious sunshine in an otherwise dull day, an impressive
and magnificent spectacle. The King remained with his
hand at the salute, while I gave: 'The Parade will slope
and order arms and stand-at-ease.' Then I trotted out
towards him, and he trotted out towards me, extending

his hand as he came near, with a cheery winning smile. 'How do you do, General,' he said in a deep, clear, vibrating voice, 'I am so very glad to be able to come down to see you all. It is the first time I have been able to see Australian troops in England. Shall we go up to the right of the line?'

As we turned our horses towards the right of the line three-quarters of a mile away where the Artillery were drawn up, he said: 'You used to command the 4th Brigade, didn't you? They've done awfully well. I hear you were on Gallipoli all the time. That was splendid.' Then, glancing at my ribbons: 'I'm sorry I haven't had a chance of giving you your Order. Won't you come up to Windsor some day to lunch and I'll give it to you? See Wigram about it, won't you, and fix a day to suit yourself, when you can get away.'

In short he was chatty and breezy and merry all the time, and hardly waited for me to answer him before he went on: 'How do you like my horse? He's an Australian, too! I bought him in India, just a common Australian waler. I hope it's going to keep fine. Have the men all got overcoats?' When I told him they had, and also waterproof capes, he said: 'That's fine. It always pays to look after the men's comfort, doesn't it!'

Then he said: 'Let's trot along, so that I'll have more time to look at them.' As we approached the artillery he asked a lot of questions about the supply of horses, guns and wagons, sights and harness.

As we rode at a walking pace down the whole line, nearly two miles long, I told him where each battalion or battery was raised, and he was always ready with an appropriate comment. He asked me what part of Australia I came from, and said he'd been in Melbourne twice, and that it was a fine city. Had he met me there? He said he remembered the Marquis of Linlithgow's reception in Melbourne quite well. As we rode along, he constantly referred to the question of warm clothing, saying: 'Take my advice, and make sure you get the best of woollen warm clothing. It's really very cold in France in the winter.'

When we came to the end of the 3rd Division, and to where Sir Newton Moore's troops started, he stopped and looked back and said: 'Well, General, I heartily congratulate you. It's a fine division. I don't know that I've ever seen a finer one. The men look just splendid, and so soldierly and steady.' I continued to ride with him to the extreme end of the line, when he said: 'I should like to see them march past now. Shall I go to the flagstaff?' While he trotted across to the saluting point, I and my staff went full gallop across the front of the parade, where the head of the artillery had already wheeled up to the saluting base, and the sixteen bands had already passed through the line and posted themselves opposite the flag – a band of 384 performers. We placed ourselves at the head of the column, Eric leading, next Jackson and Farmar, then myself, and fifty yards behind me Grimwade and staff leading the artillery – ten mounted and six dismounted batteries and the Division Ammunition Column, 600 strong. I gave the signal to advance, and then commenced a march which continued without a break for nearly two hours.

As I wheeled around after passing the saluting

point, and reined up alongside the King, he turned to
me with a broad smile, and said: 'And yet the Germans
say we've no ear for music. Listen to those beautiful
bands. How their instruments shine, too!' His interest in
each body of troops, as they passed, was intimate and
sustained, showing that he was really interested. He did
not once take his eyes off the troops, and asked hundreds
of questions and criticized dozens of small details, such
as the quality of the artillery horses, the relative utility of
leather or web equipment, the rifles, the clothing, the
hats, the platoon commanders and their training, and so
on and on. He talked nearly all the time, jumping from
subject to subject, every now and then breaking off to
mutter 'Splendid, splendid!'

He told me he had reviewed already 1,500,000
men since the war began, adding with special emphasis:
'Isn't it perfectly wonderful. No man could have done it
but Lord K. People kept saying he was going to work in
the wrong way, but he knew better. He was right after
all.'

Then suddenly changing the subject: 'Did you
meet my son out in Egypt? He wrote and told me how
good all you Australians had been to him.' He made one
remark commencing: 'If we win this war …' and I
smiled and said: '*If* we win?' Whereupon he threw back
his head and laughed a full laugh and said: 'Oh yes! We'll
win right enough; nobody need make any mistake
about that.' Then: 'The Germans started out to smash
the British Empire! – smash it to pieces – and look, just
look' – with a sweep of his arm up and down the
marching columns – 'see what they've really done.

They've made an empire of us' ...

Again, as the long column came to an end, he turned to me with shining eyes and said – 'Perfectly splendid, magnificent!' I then presented to him my brigadiers, and battery and battalion commanders, and then we rode down together to the Bulford station, about a mile away, I riding on the right of the King, the Royal Standard behind us, and the rest of our retinues following. And then came the climax of it all. For I had the troops drawn up, closely packed together one hundred deep, on the sloping field adjoining the road, and, as the King rode by, each unit broke into deafening cheer upon cheer, raising hats aloft on bayonets. It was a stirring sight, and our horses, though made jumpy, behaved splendidly.

The King rode with his head bowed, looking grave and solemn, and when he had passed the last of the troops, he turned to me and said – 'It makes a lump come in my throat, to think of all these splendid fellows coming all those many thousands of miles; and what they have come for.' And he said not another word till we reached the station where he dismounted ... I forgot to mention that the first thing he did when he dismounted was to take a lump of sugar out of his pocket and give it to his horse.

Now that is the story of the review, and it will be a red-letter day to all who were present. As soon as the King left, the weather broke and the rain came down in sheets, so that we all got thoroughly soaked riding and marching home to camp ...

Lark Hill, 10 October 1916

Since last writing, I have for the first time since 25 July run up to the War Office on official business. Enclosed herewith is a card of Mme Vigee le Brun's painting of herself which I got at the National Gallery, where I spent Saturday afternoon, and which you will remember we did not visit when in London. The original painting is one I greatly admired, and is executed in much the same style as her painting of self and child in the Louvre. The National is the only gallery in London now open. Most of the others have the pictures stowed in cellars for fear of Zepps. The same applied to the Abbey, where also most of the statuary which could not be stored is covered with heaps of sandbags.

By today's post I am sending you a small parcel containing two souvenirs, no less than pieces of the aluminium framework of the Zepp which was shot down and landed almost intact on the east coast of Essex. I got these from Walter [Dr Rosenhain, Monash's brother-in-law], who has been commissioned to analyse the metal, and who personally selected these (among other) specimens. So you have an actual piece of the aerial monster which came out of Germany, and which will be renowned in history. There is much competition here for the tiniest genuine scrap of the leviathan …

I was astonished in London at the large number of work-women wearing trousers or breeches – lamp-cleaners, bill-posters, taxi-drivers, bus-conductors, ticket-collectors, message-girls. Of course many wear short navy-blue skirts, but trousers seem to be the most common.

The business which took me up to London related
to the equipping of the 3rd Division, and I have at last
got a promise from Sir William Robertson [the Chief of
the Imperial General Staff] that mine would be the next
division to be equipped and sent abroad. I have nothing
definite to go on, but I calculate that any time after four
weeks from now we may be close to a move. It will take
quite that time, at the least, to get together the rest of the
guns, machine-guns, vehicles, horses and rifles ...

Darrington, 21 November 1916

All who have a right to be called 'Anzacs' among us are
now wearing a metal 'A' on the colour patches on the
sleeves.

The division started to move at five o'clock this
morning by train to Southampton and thence by ship to
Havre and Rouen. It will take eighty-seven railway
trains, each of about thirty coaches and trucks, to move
the whole division, and the move is spread over six days.
Everything has been most carefully timed, and up to
now nearly twenty trains have left Amesbury punctually
and without a hitch.

With one A.D.C. and the senior staff officer of
each branch, together with four batmen and two clerks,
I shall leave Charing Cross at 8.20 a.m. on Saturday
25 November and proceed via Folkestone to Boulogne
where three cars will meet us.

From all sides one hears encomiums of the division. The War Office authorities say that it is 'the best
equipped division that has ever left England'. Southern
Command say it is the best trained division that has left

since the Old Army disappeared. I only hope they will
live up to their reputation. You should have heard the
men cheering as train after train went out today.

France, 7 December 1916

I am installed in full command of nearly 5 per cent of
the whole of the British Line, with jurisdiction over an
enormous area, including two large towns, a dozen
smaller villages, and hundreds of hamlets, with control
over the civil population as well. My headquarters are in
a chateau in the town of Steenwerck. The chateau is
modern and well-equipped, with electric light, hot-
water service, and large grounds with stables and garages
attached. The owner is a captain in the French Army,
and his family still occupy a part of the house, while
Jackson, Farmar, Eric and myself and our batmen
occupy the remainder ...

France, 21 December 1916

A visit today from the Commander-in-Chief, Sir Douglas Haig. I turned out the whole of my reserve brigade,
and detachments from all the other units of the division,
and the C-in-C rode around with me and had a look at
them.

Douglas Haig looked grey and old. On parting he
put his arm around my shoulder (as I rode beside him)
and with much feeling and warmth he said – 'You have
a very fine division. I wish you all sorts of good luck, old
man.' I was surprised when he told me he'd been in Australia. [Haig had visited Australia in 1892 while on leave
from his regiment in India.]

France, 11 January 1917

Ever since I got back to France I have been trying to
find time to write you a little by way of description of
the activities of a division at the front, as exemplified by
the doings of my division for the past seven weeks. I
suppose the popular idea of the public as to the doings
of the army in France is that there is one or at most two
rows of deep trenches all along the front, in which we
stand glaring at the enemy standing in a similar trench
on the other side of a strip of territory called no man's
land – all our people (and his) standing side by side, if
not shoulder to shoulder, and throwing things at him,
and trying to dodge the things he throws at us. Holding
the line does not mean anything like this at all, for the
great bulk of our activities, measured both by numbers
employed and by their importance, has very little to do
with the front-line trenches.

The whole of my sector, which is nearly five out of
the ninety-two miles of the British front, is actually held
defensively by only one platoon of each of four companies, of each of four battalions, while all the other nine
battalions, all the artillery and engineers, and all the
administrative services, have all sorts of work to do
which not only has nothing to do with the trenches, but
often takes them many miles in the rear. The front line
is not really a line at all, but a very complex and elaborate system of field works, extending back several
thousand yards, and bristling with fire trenches, support,
and communication trenches, redoubts, strong points,
machine-gun emplacements, and an elaborate system of
dugouts, cabins, posts and observation cells. Life in the

front system is very arduous and uncomfortable, and a front-line battalion stays in only six days, during which each platoon is changed round, so that at the worst a single man seldom does more than forty-eight hours continuous front trench duty in every twelve days, and every forty-eight days the whole brigade gets relieved by the reserve brigade and goes out for a complete rest, or for work in the back area, for a clear twenty-four days. At least, all this is in my particular system — designed to spread the stress on the personnel as widely as possible ...

The Artillery are the only ones who have scarcely anything else to do but to fight and shoot, but even they have constant work, not only in their own maintenance, and that of their wagon-lines and horses (in some cases miles in rear), but also in the upkeep and repair of their gunpits and guns and ammunition. The divisional area extends back from the front upwards of twenty miles, and my responsibilities include the administration of the whole area and all the civil and military population which it contains, including as you already know one large town, partly in ruins.

The infantry offensive action consists of patrols, who creep right up to the enemy lines and bomb them, and in continual raids, one every two or three days, from fifty to three hundred men strong. We kill a good many Boches and bring back always a good deal of loot and sometimes a few prisoners. The other night Lieutenant Jewkes got five of them in a dugout calling 'Kamerad'. He came up to take their surrender, when one of them fired point-blank and hit him in the head. Jewkes has since died – so have the five Boches. They went a good many feet into the air when our gun-cotton sent them and dugout all up together.

The big question is, of course, the food and ammunition supply, the former term covering meat, bread, groceries, hay, straw, oats, wood, coal, paraffin and candles, the latter comprising cartridges, shells, shrapnel, bombs, grenades, flares, and rockets. It takes a couple of thousand men and horses with hundreds of wagons, and 118 huge motor lorries, to supply the daily wants of my population of 20,000. My railhead, Steenwerck, is at any hour of the day a far busier sight than the Spencer Street Station goods-yards, and all the work has to be done in mud and slush. For hours every morning the roads – and the French roads are very narrow and very bad – are congested with interminable lines of four-mule wagons, waiting their turn for their loads. Can you picture the careful organization required to ensure that all these supplies, which are daily loaded on to trains at the sea base, should punctually reach the cooking-pot, or mess-tin of every man of the division, wherever he may be? Much of our distribution has to be done at night – for safety – in horrible weather, and much of it (within a couple of miles of the front trenches) on men's backs, because trenches are not big and wide enough for vehicles of any kind. Similarly the ammunition has to be distributed, each kind to its appointed dump or magazine, in such quantities as I may order to be used from day to day. For we dare not create large stores within range of enemy guns, for fear a chance shell may blow them up. Our large dumps are away back and vulnerable only to aeroplane bombs. With reference to food we also have to see that all the men in the front lines regularly get hot food – coffee, oxo, porridge, stews. They cannot cook it themselves, for at the least sight of the smoke of a fire the spot is instantly shelled. And they must get it regularly or they would perish of cold or frostbite, or get 'trench feet', which occasionally means amputation. So I have got the pioneers to make hundreds of 'Thermos Flasks', boxes lined with straw into which the 'dixies' or cooking-pots can be packed, and these are carried on men's backs up to the forward defences, the food remaining quite hot.

It is also imperative to attend to the men's boots and socks. A special oganization looks after the collection of wet socks from men in the trenches, and these are taken down to the divisional baths to be washed and dried, and clean dry socks are daily sent up in sacks, by platoons. The boots I refer to are special trench boots called gum-boots, made of rubber up to the thighs. I have 6,000 on hand of which 3,000 are in use, while the other 3,000 are back out of the line, in the 'Gum-Boots Store' where there are drying rooms; this establishment being run by a special detail of men ...

I only wish I had not this large town on my hands, it gives me more work and trouble than all the rest of the division – although, of course, I can, in a quiet way get a lot of good derelict materials – bricks, timber, fuel, electric bells and wire, stoves, chairs, tables, and other things my infantry and artillery covet – that is, when my own police are not too alert in arresting, as I order them to do, any persons looting deserted houses in pursuance of my own orders. My signal officer wanted a new dynamo the other day, for the lighting-plant of my chateau. I told him where I had seen one, in a deserted factory in Armentières (into one shed of which we are putting in a battery, of four and a half inch howitzers). Could he take it? Well, yes, provided Major Dering did not catch him taking it. If he allowed his men to be caught they would have to be tried for looting! ...

I have two divisional baths, one at Steenwerck, one at Pont de Nieppe, a suburb of the large town. In these are washed 2,000 men daily, with hot water in great brewery tubs. Each man hands in his old under clothes and gets in exchange a complete clean outfit. I employ over 200 girls in the laundries washing and ironing the soiled clothes. It is quite a show sight, but how they live and work all day in steam so thick that they can't see six feet in front of them, I don't know ...

In the *École Professionelle* in Armentières, or so much of it as is left after the aeroplane bomb had hit it a few months ago, I run a 'Grand cinema show and pierrot entertainment', charging the lads half a franc admission. They appreciate it all the more if they are compelled to pay – wouldn't trouble to come if it were free. The hall, once an engineering lecture theatre, holds five hundred. The whole thing is under the management of [Frank] Beaurepaire [the world champion swimmer] who is my head Y.M.C.A. representative ...

The pierrots (eight of them) all have splendid voices, and all turn out in white pierrot gear, three of them as fair damsels, all the clothes made by our regimental tailors, and they give a show every bit as good as those at St Kilda. Each of my thirteen bands furnishes the orchestra each evening in rotation. General Godley and I make a point of going to this show about once a week. It bucks the men up a lot after six days' tour in the trenches. Many of the songs and jokes are topical, very personal and very funny, take too long to tell you, some directed against Godley and me and the brigadiers, but they are in very good taste, and quite respectful, and the men simply roar with delight.

Menton, 14 March 1917

Doubtless you will stare at the above address and wonder how I got here, and why. Well, I had been fighting the question of leave for the division for some time, but the difficulties are great. In an army of 2,000,000 if everyone is to have even only one week's leave in the year that means that 40,000 men would have to get leave every day [*sic*]. Imagine what cross-Channel shipping that would require! It was recently decided that none were to get leave from France, until all those who had had no leave for over twelve months had had their turn. This, of course, put the 3rd Division clean out of it. I then raised the question in regard to about 100 officers and men, who, like myself, had joined the division from France or Egypt, and upon this the corps commander sent for me, and told me that no one in the division deserved leave more than I did and that I had better take ten days at once, and on my return I might grant similar leave to a selected few, as and when I could spare them. So I made my arrangements, leaving General Jobson in command, and came away last Friday, 9th instant.

On this occasion I shall write nothing whatever
about the 3rd Division or its recent doings. I want to try
here to forget all about my ordinary environment for a
few days.

The train for Paris was crowded and late and mis-
erably slow. All *trains de luxe* and *trains rapides* have, of
course, disappeared and it was midnight before I got
into the Gare du Nord, and to an hotel. My stay in Paris
covered two days and one night. It snowed all the time
and the streets were a slough of mud and slush. One
lunch I had at Maxim's in the Rue Royale (close to La
Madeleine). Its glory has indeed departed – no band, no
music, everything very drab – even women waitresses –
yet they served a nice lunch, for the Parisian chef knows
how to dish up the plainest food. I wonder do you really
realize the privations of war! No butter, very little sugar,
all the beautiful French fancy bread and rolls are gone,
and in their stead is a coarse, brown kind of bread. Fresh
bread is forbidden to be sold, yet it is crisp and palatable,
and better than the spongy, doughy stuff we get at the
front. No potatoes – everything at more than double the
ordinary prices. As advised by Dering I took all my four
meals in Paris at various restaurants and found the Café
de la Paix, near the Place de l'Opéra, much the best. I
thus had a chance of watching Parisian life, in a quiet
way. What impressed me was the entire absence of
'side'. There is absolutely no difference in the manners
and style of the waiter, or the French officer of high
rank, or the patrician dame, or the girl who checks your
tickets in the Metro (underground), or the taxi-driver,
or the poilu (French soldier). There is a wonderful

camaraderie and *égalite* [*sic*], yet withal a marvellous politeness. The politeness of the French to each other and to strangers is remarkable. The commonest person will use the politest words and the politest actions on each and all occasions. These characteristics of human comradeship and gentle amiability are what appeal to me so much with the French. Life in the cafes is remarkably free from restraint. Waiters chat familiarly with officers of high rank in uniform; but don't forget that the waiters are only soldiers who have fought and been wounded and have been granted a month or two 'permission' for convalescence, after discharge from hospital. Everybody talks to everybody else. Obvious strangers argue the news of the day together. Of course the great bulk of the patrons of the cafes are men in uniform – chiefly officers blazing with decorations; and their deference to an Australian major-general is most embarrassing …

The army in France is a glorious army. Its camaraderie, its prestige, its spirit and endurance, its morale and confidence are wonderful. It is an army – British, Ausralian, Canadian and French – united in a bond of fellowship such as there never was before in all history, and it is something to have lived for, and something to remember for the rest of one's days, to have held a high command in such an army. But there, I am getting back to the war, and must sheer off.

Menton, 16 March 1917

You say I might take up military work as a profession after the war? I hate the business of war, the horror of it, the waste, the destruction, and the inefficiency. Many a time I could have wished that wounds or sickness, or a breakdown of health would have enabled me to retire honourably from the field of action – like so many other senior officers. My only consolation has been the sense of faithfully doing my duty to my country, which has placed a grave responsibility upon me, and to my division which trusts and follows me, and I owe something to the 20,000 men whose lives and honour are placed in my hands to do with as I will. But my duty once done, and honourably discharged, I shall, with a sigh of relief, turn my back once and for all on the possibility of ever again having to go through such an awful time ...

The Front, 24 March 1917

Back here with the 3rd Division, I have still further increased my frontage, and I am now holding, in addition to the sectors previously described, the whole of Ploegsteert (Plugstreet) wood and the historic Hill 63. We are in the midst of active preparations for an operation which will give the Boche as nasty a knock as he has yet had anywhere.

Monash witnessed the launching on 9 April 1917 of the great British offensive from Arras by two British armies, principally Allenby's Third Army, which was timed to precede by one week an equally massive French offensive on the Aisne. The Battle of Arras began brilliantly, following a five-day bombardment of the enemy lines by two million shells, and at its outset achieved complete surprise; Vimy Ridge was seized by the Canadian Corps on the first day and the initial advance, accompanied by tanks, was deep. But German counter-attacks were swiftly mounted and within days Allenby's control of the battle was lost. Advancing divisions were marooned and overwhelmed; reinforcements were unable to reach them in time and within a week the remaining tanks and the offensive itself were floundering in the mud: British losses by early May reached nearly 160,000 men. The great French offensive launched on the Aisne front on 16 April met a similar fate, without even achieving surprise, and the slaughter in the first week led to widespread mutinies in an already exhausted French Army, the repercussions of which were to paralyse France's war effort for a year.

26 April 1917

The Vimy battle [the Arras offensive] took place within earshot of here. I went down to see the early stages of it. At night, for many nights past, the southern sky is lit up as if by a bushfire, and the roar of the guns has been continuous for days …

Have you heard of the glorious doings of the old 4th Brigade? They broke through the Hindenburg Line but suffered heavily, The Chief [Field-Marshal Sir Douglas Haig] describes it as the finest feat of the war.

As part of the Battle of Arras, the 4th Australian Division, then serving in General Gough's Fifth Army, south of Third Army, was ordered against the fortified village of Bullecourt on 11 April. It took part of the Hindenburg Line without the assistance of tanks (which broke down) or artillery, but suffered grievously before it was withdrawn next day. Monash's old 4th Brigade alone lost 2,339 of its 3,000 men, and this tragic loss appalled him. Bullecourt was finally taken on 20 May. At this

stage Monash's personal letters become shorter and less fre-
quent, for his attentions are now fully engaged in the fighting.

3rd Aust. Div. H.Q., France,
29 April 1917 (midnight)
[To his business associate, John Gibson of Melbourne]

My dear Gibson,

I find it very difficult to write connectedly on any
matter not directly associated with my present activities.
The Arras battle is at its height. Ever since 5 April the
roar has never ceased day or night; my duty has been to
keep the enemy opposed to me on my present front,
pinned to his ground, and the back areas are alive with
troops moving into and out of the battle. So far the role
assigned to my division in the mosaic of events has been
an ancillary and subordinate one, but that is chiefly
because, in the tests which have been applied by the
Commander-in-Chief to the calibre of this division
during the last five months since I brought it to the
front, we have come out so brilliantly, that we and certain few other divisions have been specially earmarked
for the still greater and culminating offensive plan which
is to mark this year's campaign. Active preparations for
this have been in hand for many weeks, and it is now
only a question of waiting for the psychological
moment.

I wonder if it is possible for you to realize the scope
and scale and dynamic splendour of a modern battle. No
mere words can convey any idea of it, or of the complexity of the organization and administrative detail

required to co-ordinate the action of the 20,000 people and all their different weapons, guns, howitzer, trench-mortars, bombs, rifles machine-guns, tanks, aeroplanes, balloons, mines, etc. I leave you to imagine the sense of responsibility which weighs upon one charged with the duty of wielding this tremendous weapon just in the right way and in the right time and place quite apart from the task of bringing it fit and fed and rested and in fighting spirit to the battle-front when and where required ...

For myself I am very heartily sick of the whole war business. Its horror, its ghastly inefficiency, its unspeakable cruelty and misery have always appalled me, but there is nothing to do but to set one's teeth and stick it out as long as one can ...

France, 15 May 1917

You have no doubt heard all about the brilliant work done by Birdwood's Corps (1st Anzac) at Bullecourt, where they have broken through the Hindenburg Line. All this is in the Fifth Army.

Have you heard how well Harry Chauvel has done? Report says he saved the situation at Gaza [in Egypt], which was nearly a disaster for our arms. Rumour has it that he will be given command of a mounted corps in Egypt with the rank of lieutenant-general. Imagine an Australian rising to the rank of corps commander ...

Monash was now preparing for his 3rd Division's first experi-
ence of battle. With the New Zealand Division it formed the

nucleus of II Anzac Corps under Godley and the Corps
(which included the 25th British Division) was destined to be
the principal instrument in gaining the first great British
victory of the war on the Western Front: the capture of
Messines-Wytschaete Ridge. Its architect was the commander
of Second Army, General Sir Herbert Plumer, who was blessed
with a gifted Chief of Staff, 'Tim' Harington; they were steady,
cautious men who for more than a year had been planning the
elimination of the German salient south of Ypres, the backbone
of which lay on the Messines ridge. They informed Monash of
their plans on 7 March. They would use their three Corps –
IX and X British and II Anzac – advancing in high summer
over firm ground. More than twenty huge tunnels were stealth-
ily dug under the ridge and filled with explosive. The attacking
troops were trained in advancing over terrain almost identical to
the ground they would have to cover, and shown detailed scale
models of the defences. Monash worked out his own intricate
plans for his division, a document he called his 'Magnum
Opus', and gave copies of it to his brigadiers on 15 April. The
Australian Official Historian, Charles Bean, commented that
'there was concentrated upon the plans an amount of thought
and care far beyond that ever devoted to any other scheme of
operations produced by a staff of the AIF'. Monash pored over
aerial photographs of the defences, noting every enemy trench
and gun emplacement, and worked out timetables for their
elimination.

France, 19 May 1917

I am now in the thick of preparation for our forth-
coming offensive operations. My job is to capture
the southern spur of a famous ridge, and to form a

defensive flank for our army. For weeks past, we have been making roads, building railways and tramways, forming ammunition-dumps, making gun emplacements and camouflaging them, preparing brigade and battalion battle headquarters and laying a complex system of underground cables, fixing the positions of machine-guns, heavy guns and howitzers. For this operation I shall have added to my own artillery five army brigades of field artillery. The heavy and siege artillery will not be under my command. Then there is a mass of field engineering work to be done, in large dugouts, approach-avenues, assembly and jumping-off trenches; most voluminous orders to be got out, controlling the action of the whole of my 20,000 men and animals – feeding organization, transport organization, ammunition supply, cutting the enemy's wire (an operation now in full blast), the preliminary destructive bombardment of his field works, the completion and blowing up of mines, and finally the preparation of the 12,000 infantry, for the actual work of 'going over the top'.

The Army commander [General Plumer] spent all yesterday afternoon with me, going patiently and minutely through the whole of my plans, and said he felt sure that I had done all that was possible to ensure success.

Long before this letter reaches you the attack will be over and the 3rd Division will either have achieved a brilliant success or else got a bad hammering. But I have every confidence in the men, and I know they have in me.

The 10th Brigade is doing fine, though it would be

invidious to make any distinction between the brigades. I regard the 9th Brigade (Jobson) as the best lot of men, the 10th (McNicoll) as the best trained and most soldierly, and the 11th (Cannan) as the best individual fighters. But they are all three good in all aspects. The 10th Brigade have won many more distinctions since I wrote you of them last. The four battalions of the 10th are now commanded by 37th Smith, 38th Davis, 39th Henderson, 40th Lord (Chief Commissioner of Police Tasmania).

The ridge was bombarded for seven days before the offensive. At 3.10 a.m., 7 June 1917, the mines were detonated with an explosion that could be heard in England, and following a perfectly placed moving barrage, Second Army advanced, with 3rd Australian Division and New Zealand Division on their northern (left) flank moving forward with clockwork precision through a hail of gas shells, taking all their objectives. At 3 p.m. Phase Two began and 4th Australian Division took over the Australian offensive. German counter-attacks lasted until 11 June, along with incessant bombardment of the ground lost, and British casualties totalled 26,000 of whom 12,000 were Anzacs. But Messines was a victory, complete if costly, and Monash, who was flattered by the personal congratulations of Haig, Plumer and Godley for his division's role, wrote: 'I am the greatest possible believer in the theory of the limited objective.' His heavy casualties to German shellfire made him wonder if someday he could advance deeply and rapidly enough to capture the enemy gun line.

France, 7 June 1917

My message to the division: 'I desire to convey my gratitude to all commanders and all troops of the division for the magnificent valour and splendid co-operation, as well as the high technical skill which all ranks and all arms and departments have displayed in the achievement of this day's great victory. It now only remains to show that the division is just as well able to hold on to what it has won, and is more than a match for the enemy in the hastily improvised defensive.'

A great victory (Messines), thoroughly defeated the 4th Bavarian Division (under Prince Franz) and the 3rd Bavarian Division (my old antagonists east of Armentières). These divisions practically blotted out, as far as infantry is concerned, both opposite my sector.

On my left the New Zealanders had Saxons and Wurttemburgers, who also got a bad beating. Farther north, Prussians.

My losses about 2,000. The division captured altogether eleven field-guns, over fifty machine-guns, and many trench mortars, munitions, and the like. Many others were smashed to splinters, and the majority still lie buried in the wreckage of the enemy defences.

I fired from first to last over 1,000,000 [pounds] worth of ammunition, large and small, in the three days' fighting.

France, 26 July 1917

I don't know what they tell the relatives of men who are shot for desertion or cowardice. Probably the truth.

As you no doubt know, the Australian Government

will not agree to the death sentence being carried into effect in the A.I.F. This is having a very bad effect on discipline. I have had no single case in 3rd Division, but now, while acting as corps commander, I have recently confirmed six death sentences in 4th Division, but they have had to be commuted to ten years' penal servitude. Only today I had a long talk with the army commander (Sir Herbert Plumer) about it, and I am writing to Pearce to urge strongly that in some clear case of cowardly desertion, the law should take its course.

The term 'duty in the trenches' is a very loose one. It does not mean actually in a trench in the ground. The whole area for several miles behind our front outpost line is subject to shell-fire, and the whole of a division which happens to be 'in line' may be regarded as 'in the trenches'.

It is quite a mistake to regard Frenchmen, as a nation, as being short and of poor physique. This does apply to the Belgians, but the French are for the most part tall, handsome, and graceful, and if short, are usually very sturdy.

The 6th Division is still 'training' in England, only two brigades have so far been formed. It seems very unlikely in the present state of recruiting, that the 6th Division will ever come to France, but more than likely will be broken up to reinforce the other five divisions, as has happened in the Canadian force. [The 6th Division never took the field. After the failure of Prime Minister Hughes' efforts via referenda in 1916 and 1917 to introduce conscription in Australia, its units were used as reinforcements for the other five Australian divisions, which remained the only all-volunteer army on the Western Front.]

France, 3 August 1917

Our part in the great attack of 31 July [in the Third battle of Ypres] was only a subsidiary operation, and I employed only two battalions. This was carried out chiefly as a feint on Warneton and fully achieved its purpose. Our main attack was, of course, as is now known, north of Ypres. It has been raining heavily and incessantly for three days, and the condition of the forward battle zone is unspeakable. Our people are in mud and water up to their waists. Everything is hung up in consequence ...

France, 6 August 1917

My division is now, at last, due for a short rest, and is to be replaced by the 4th (Maclagan). The process of relief usually takes nearly a week, and the first stages have begun. As part of this process the 4th Brigade (Brand) has come temporarily under my command, and I have put it into the line to relieve one of my own brigades. The 1st Anzac Corps is now in this vicinity – with the divisions of Walker, Smyth, and Hobbs; and in consequence I have seen a good deal of Birdwood and Brudenell White. [It is worth noting that of these five generals Monash mentions, only White was an Australian.] Birdwood told me the Commander-in-Chief [Haig] had a very high opinion of my division and of me personally, and had gone out of his way to express himself in terms of praise of my work. B. added that it

was rare for the Chief to do this. White entirely confirmed these statements. There are other evidences on
which to judge that special attention is being given to
my division, as regards refitting and recruitment. For
example, Sir H. Plumer told me yesterday the Chief had
taken steps to get this division brought up again to full
war strength as soon as possible (we being now 2,500
below war strength). All this means something abnor-
mal. There have been vague rumours for some time in
well-informed circles of a contemplated regrouping of
the Australian forces. It has even been suggested that B.
may get an army command.

France, 16 August 1917

In recent weeks, as I think I told you, the whole of the
other Australians have come up into this district, and I
have been able to exchange visits with some of my old
friends. Thus, the whole five divisions are, for the time
being, much closer together, and an immense territory
extending back twenty-five miles from the line has
every village full of Australian troops ... This morning I
was up at 3 a.m., and with two of my staff went about
five miles north and climbed the Scherpenberg (Belgium) and from it at 4.45 a.m. witnessed the opening of
the second phase of the great Ypres battle. The spectacle in the early dawn of the opening of our artillery
barrage on a front of fifteen miles from Ypres to the sea
was magnificent and terrifying, putting into the shade
the most terrible lightning and thunderstorm ever witnessed. The whole country simply trembled. Accounts
coming in show that all goes well ...

France, 10 September 1917

We were very fortunate in striking, without being aware of it, a charity fete in the form of a Military Horse Show, in the beautiful grounds of the Casino, and it was there that we spent the afternoon. The 'show' was confined to officers' chargers, who were shown with owners up, over a course of hunting jumps and obstacles under Olympia rules. The ground, with a background of beautiful forest all around it, is only small, and provides room for not more than 300 or 400 spectators; but such a cosmopolitan and motley crowd it would be difficult to find anywhere − French and English ladies, selling programmes and tickets and sweets, and wearing committee and Red Cross badges; smart Belgian Dragoon officers, with clanking sabres and orange facings to their collars and cuffs; young English flappers in the smart uniform of the Women's Auxiliary Army Corps who act as clerks, car-drivers, waitresses and messengers; French officers, as always, wearing all their decorations and medals; Canadian nurses who have a kind of military uniform with badges of rank of captains and majors on their shoulders; a group of Indian native officers of the Lahore Lancers, beturbaned and wearing costly jewels; Chinese coolies in smart blue smocks, gigantic fellows, looking clean and soldierly; numbers of Portuguese offices and soldiers coming to 'barrack' for their compatriots (for the Portuguese is a fine horseman); a sprinkling of United States officers and soldiers of the new Army, just landed; numerous officers of the Imperial Army − English, Irish, Scotch, Australian, and New Zealand − mostly convalescents from the local rest homes; a sprinkling of smart young Parisiennes, immaculately and daintily gowned and hatted; a few burly Russian soldiers, tall and bearded; and a crowd of British and Indian Lancers, French Cuirassiers, and Australian Light Horsemen ...

The victory of Messines formed a prelude to the series of offensives known as the Third Battle of Ypres, launched by Haig to secure the rail junction at Roulers, only twenty kilometres from the British front, clear the Channel coast, and wear down the dwindling strength of the German Army. The first offensive began on 31 July, in high summer, but unseasonal rain fell on the first day, turning the flat, featureless, sandy earth of Flanders into mud. By the end of August the British had lost 67,000 men, for little gain of ground, but Haig ordered the offensives to continue under the command of Plumer, the master of the 'step-by-step' advance under strong artillery barrage. On 20 September I Anzac Corps entered battle, taking Menin Road Ridge, and on 26 September the newly arrived 4th and 5th Australian Divisions captured Polygon Wood; each advance had cost more than 5,000 casualties, but German losses were also high.

France, 24 September 1917

You will have heard by now that the campaign for the Passchendaele Ridge (which I foreshadowed in a recent letter), started on the 20th. 1st Anzac (which has again resumed the 4th Division) is having the first go, and we (2nd Anzac) shall come in later. 1st and 2nd Divisions did the first 'push' most brilliantly; day after to-morrow 4th and 5th Divisions will come through them and to a second push; and early in October, self and Russell (N.Z.) Expect to capture the Gravenstafel Spur, and later on get right on to the Passchendaele Ridge proper. Godley's corps will temporarily comprise six divisions, and by a curious coincidence my division will take over its sector from the 3rd Division which is one of the original 'First Seven Divisions' of the original British Army. The fighting done in this 'push' by the Australians has been most brilliant in every way.

My move will take five days, and it will be hard marching all the time, but the men are very fit, and I am again up to full war strength. We have been doing four weeks' reorganization and training in most beautiful rolling country, mostly in beautiful autumn sunshine, and we finished up last Saturday with a splendid review by the Commander-in-Chief, who motored over from his advanced H.Q. (which is only twenty miles from me) sending his horses ahead. I paraded 12,000 troops (but no transport) and the whole show was a brilliant success. The Chief stayed for an hour after the last troops had passed, chatting to me and my senior commanders …

On 1 October 1917 Monash arrived at Ypres in Belgium, to plan his division's part in the third step, the capture of Brood-seinde Ridge east of Ypres. In the coming battle, scheduled for 4 October, divisions from the two Anzac corps would be fighting side by side for the first time in the war. Note that Monash uses the address 'France' in the next few letters, possibly for security reasons, when he is obviously writing from Ypres.

France, 1 October 1917

I am writing in a dugout in the eastern ramparts of
Ypres, close to the Menin Gate – I don't know what this
conveys to you. I'm afraid it would be impossible
to convey anything like a true picture of the situation.
To begin with, you probably know that until the beginning of the great Flanders offensive of 1917, and ever
since the close of the second battle of Ypres in 1915, this
town has lain under easy reach of the Boche guns,
and has been subjected to constant shelling every day
and every night. Ypres was an old walled town and
encircled by ramparts, which presented a sufficient
thickness of breastworks to be fairly safe against enemy
shells. Under and in the sides of these ramparts numerous tunnelled dugouts, cabins, and galleries have been
constructed during the three years that the British have
been defending the town.

In one considerable group of such tunnels, just near
the Menin Gate, I have established my battle headquarters for the next phase of the battle of Ypres. It is in
every respect like the underground workings of mines,
narrow tunnels, broadening out here and there into little
chambers, the whole lit by electric light, run by my own
portable electric plant. It is cold and dank and overrun
by rats and mice, and altogether smelly and disagreeable,
but here I shall have to stay for nearly three weeks.
Myself, A.D.C.s staff, clerks, signallers, cooks, batmen
and attached officers are tucked away all over the place,
in little cabins, recesses, and dugouts. Our A mess is just
like a little cabin of a sailing ship or tramp steamer, and
there is scarcely room to move anywhere.

The town of Ypres, once a marvel of medieval architectural beauty, lies all around us a stark, pitiable ruin. You are doubtless already familiar with pictures showing bits of it. For three years it has been dying a lingering death, and now there is nothing left of its fine streets, its great square, its cathedral, the historic Cloth Hall, its avenues, and boulevards of fine mansions, its hospitals, its town hall, or its straggling suburbs, but a charred collection of pitiable ruins — a scene of utter collapse and desolation. I am sending you herewith a characteristic postcard, and am also posting a full-page illustration from the *Sphere*. Although we have pushed back the Boche several miles east of Ypres, and most of his guns and howitzers are now beyond range, yet he still shells the town intermittently with long-range high velocity guns, and every day a few more of the gaunt, spectral pillars, which once were fine historic buildings, are toppled over and crumbled into dust. There can be little doubt that it cost the enemy in ammunition fired many times more to destroy the town than ever it cost to build it.

Difficult as it is to convey any idea of the destruction of Ypres, it is simply impossible to describe the life and turmoil in the whole area, from Poperinghe forward through Vlamertinghe (also destroyed) and Ypres, as far as our present forward position. It is one enormous medley of military activity of every conceivable description, and the traffic on the main roads is simply incredible. Imagine the traffic in Elizabeth Street for an hour after the last race on Cup Day, multiplied tenfold and extending in a continuous line from Flemington to

Sandringham, and streams of men, vehicles, motor lorries, horses, mules, and motors of every description,
moving ponderously forward, at a snail's pace, in either
direction hour after hour, all day and all night, day after
day, week after week, in never-halting never-ending
stream.

Yet in this apparent confusion and turmoil there is
order and system, and every vehicle has a definite start-
ing point, destination, and purpose. If you could stand
for half an hour at what we know as the Asylum Corner,
at the southern entrance to Ypres, where the roads from
Dickebusch and Poperinghe meet, you would see this
never-ending stream ploughing its way slowly and
painfully through the mud, man and horse plastered to
the eyes in mud, and a reek of petrol and smoke everywhere.

Here comes a body of fighting troops, tin-hatted
and fully equipped, marching in file into the battle area,
to carry out a relief of some front-line unit. There follows a string of perhaps one hundred heavy motor
lorries, all fully loaded with supplies; a limousine motor
car with some divisional staff officer; a string of regimental horse- and mule-drawn vehicles going up to a
forward transport park; some motor-ambulance wagons;
more heavy motor lorries; a long string of remount
horses, marching in twos, going up to replenish wastage;
a great 12-inch howitzer, dragged by two steam traction
engines, returning from the workshops after repair of
injuries received; more infantry, thousands of them;
more ambulances, more motor lorries, a long stream of
Chinese coolies, smart and of magnificent stature; more

lorries; every now and then a staff motor car, struggling through the melee; dozens of dispatch riders on motor bikes threading their way skilfully between the gaps; a battery of artillery all fully horsed and clattering and jingling; motor lorries again, heavily loaded with artillery ammunition; a motor car, a string of motor wagons bringing forward broken stone and road-making materials; more infantry, with a mounted police detachment mixed up with them; an 'Archie' (anti-aircraft gun), steam-motor drawn, going to take up a more forward position; more motor lorries, more artillery; every now and again a Royal Flying Corps car carrying parts of aeroplanes to forward hangars; more ambulances, and so on and on and on in a never-ending stream.

And yet all this conveys no real idea of the real thing. There has been said no truer thing than that 'war is work'.

France, 4 October 1917

I have cabled Melbourne to following effect: 'All well. Division again brilliantly victorious in "greatest battle of war".'

We have had a magnificent success, our order of battle south to north, was: 1st Australian Division, 2nd Australian Division, 3rd Australian Division, New Zealand Division.

A fine bag of prisoners is pouring in. All are most elated, particularly at the fine feat of pulling off so big a job with only three days for all our local preparation. In using the words 'greatest battle of war', I quote from a letter the Commander-in-Chief sent me yesterday.

On 4 October 1917 Monash's 3rd Division, along with the New Zealand Division, and the 1st and 2nd Australian Divisions, had taken Broodseinde Ridge — after a three-kilometre advance. Australian losses were 6,500 but the Australian Official Historian called it 'the most complete [success] ever won by the British Army in France'.

France, 7 October 1917

Handed over captured territory to 66th British Division at ten this morning, and withdrew all my infantry to rest and re-equip for the next operation a day or two after the one which will take place on 8th or 9th, leaving in all my artillery (nine brigades) and all my technical troops to prepare roads, tracks, bridges, etc., forward to the top of the ridge. Have come back myself to a little village eighteen miles from the front. Great happenings are possible in the very near future, as the enemy is terribly disorganized, and it is doubtful if his railway facilities are good enough to enable him to re-establish himself before our next two blows, which will follow very shortly and will be very severe. My next objective will be Passchendaele, unless the 66th succeed in getting so far in the next battle. The success of my division was from every point of view in the highest degree dramatic. Following a five-day's march from the back area, my task was changed at the last moment (owing to the success of the 26th), and I had only from 10 a.m. on 1 October to daybreak on 4 October to make all plans and preparations, and to bring the assault troops into their battle positions. Our success was complete and unqualified. Over 1,050 prisoners and much material and guns. Well over 1,000 dead enemy counted, and many hundreds buried and out of reach. We got absolutely astride of the main ridge. Both Corps and Army declare there has been no finer feat in the war.

The next objective for the British and Anzac divisions was the last ridge before the open country began, Passchendaele, another three kilometres distant, named after the ruins of the village on its crest. To reach Passchendaele infantry had to wade through a quagmire against the formidable obstacles of enemy block-houses and belts of barbed wire, and the attack on 12 October failed with heavy casualties.

France, 15 October 1917

Just in the degree that the battle of 4 October was brilliantly successful, so were the operations of 12 October deeply disappointing, although the 3rd Australian Division did magnificently under the most adverse circumstances.

It is bad to cultivate the habit of criticism of higher authority and, therefore, I do so now with some hesitation, but chiefly to enable you to get a correct picture of what the situation was. You will remember that the division was relieved in the line by the 66th Division, and, from the point which we had reached, viz. some 2,300 yards from Zonnebeke towards Roulers on the Zonnebeke-Roulers railway, this division was to divide with us the further advance to and inclusive of Passchendaele; each division having about a mile to go in depth. Moreover, the plan was to steadily shorten the interval of time between the successive blows. As you know, the first blow was on 20 September, the second on 26 September, the third on 4 October. Then came the necessary pause while army and corps divisional boundaries were changed, leading to the fourth blow on 9 October, and a fifth and final blow on 12 October.

I am inclined to believe that the plan was fully justified, and would have succeeded in normal weather conditions. It could only have succeeded, however, in the hands of first-class fighting divisions whose staff work was accurate, scientific and speedy. My own division and the New Zealanders had proved their ability to march for five successive days, and then go into a complex battle with only three days' preparation on the ground, and you must understand that each division has to make all its own preparations in regard to roads, tracks, pushing forward its guns, supplying its ammunition dumps, burying its telegraph cables, establishing its numerous headquarters, aid-posts and report-centres, and a thousand and one other details. We did it, as you know with complete success and perfect co-ordination in the period between 10 a.m. on 1 October and daybreak on 4 October, and the operation was a complete and perfect success. Under normal conditions we might, and probably would have, done it again in a period of forty-eight hours. But the Higher Command decided to allow us only twenty-four hours, and even under these circumstances with normal weather conditions, we might have succeeded.

However, a number of vital factors intervened, and I personally used every endeavour to secure from the corps and army commander a twenty-four hours' post-

ponement. The Chief, however, decided that every
hour's postponement gave the enemy breathing time,
and that it was worth taking the chance of achieving the
final objective for this stage of the Flanders battle.

Considerable rain began to set in on 6 October. The
ground was in a deplorable condition by the night of
8 October, and in consequence, the 66th and 45th Divisions who had taken up the role of the 3rd Australian and
the New Zealand Divisions, failed to accomplish more
than about a quarter of a mile of their projected advance.
Even in the face of this the Higher Command insisted on
going on, and insisted, further, that the uncompleted
objectives of this fourth phase should be added to
the objectives of our fifth phase; so that it amounted
to this that Russell and I were asked to make a total
advance of one and three-quarter miles [3 km].

The weather grew steadily worse on 10 and 11 October. There was no flying and no photographing, no
definite information of the German redisposition,
no effective bombardment, no opportunity of replenish-
ing our ammunition dumps; and the whole of the
country from Zonnebeke forward to the limits of our
previous captures was literally a sea of mud, in most
places waist deep. Even in spite of all these difficulties, I
might have succeeded in accomplishing the goal aimed
at but, most unfortunately, the division on my left (the
New Zealanders) had in the first stage of their advance
to cross the Ravebeek, which not only proved physically
impossible, but the banks of it had been strongly wired
on the enemy's side. Consequently, the New Zealand
Division could obtain no footing upon the Bellevue

Spur, and the left flank of my advance was, therefore, fully exposed to the enfilade fire of a large number of concrete forts scattered over the spur.

At the end of the day's operations we had accomplished only about another three-quarters of a mile of our advance, being pulled up by the exhaustion of our men within 1,000 yards of the village. My casualties have been rather heavy and will, I fear exceed 2,000, but the display of gallantry and self-devotion of the troops was altogether beyond praise. We captured 351 prisoners and did a lot of successful bayonet fighting, but on this occasion I doubt if the Boche casualties were any severer than ours. I think they were at least as severe, judging from the fact that his stretcher-parties are still at work all along our front, while our wounded have all been got in twenty-four hours ago, and the conditions of the ground which he occupies is much better than ours.

The inability to achieve the objective set is not considered in the slightest degree as a reflection upon the division and I have had the most kindly and sympathetic letters from Haig and Plumer and Godley, all saying they are more than satisfied with the work of the division, and expressing the belief that what these two divisions could not achieve no other division in the army would have been able under similar circumstances to achieve.

It has now been decided to persist in the plan and troops from another Dominion [Canadian Corps] are going to attempt it, but on this occasion ample time will be allowed for proper preparations. There will be a heavy destructive bombardment; there will be good roads and tracks made to the forward areas so as to escape the mud; all the creeks and streams will be bridged, and the job which we were asked to do in one stage will be done in three separate stages, so that the augury is all in favour of the next attempt ...

France, 18 October 1917

Our men are being put into the hottest fighting and are being sacrificed in hair-brained ventures, like Bullecourt and Passchendaele, and there is no one in the War Cabinet to lift a voice in protest. It all arises from the fact that Australia is not represented in the War Cabinet, owing to Hughes, for political reasons, having been unable to come to England. So Australian interests are suffering badly, and Australia is not getting anything like the recognition it deserves ...

The casualties are divided into 'stretcher-cases' and 'walking wounded'. All classes of case are directed by special guides, from the front of the battle to the R.A.Ps (Regimental Aid-posts), the bad cases being carried there by the regimental stretcher-bearers. Here they receive first aid. They are then taken to a collecting station further in rear, where bearers from the field ambulances carry them to the advanced dressing-station, still farther in rear. Here only the most urgent cases are redressed, the rest pass on to the main dressing-station in motor ambulances. Here a large staff of doctors and male dressers carefully examine and classify all cases, and decide on those which require operation, and these are got away first in motor ambulances, to the

C.C.S. (Casualty Clearing Station), where there are a staff of surgeons, several well-equipped theatres, and a staff of nursing sisters. After operation, inoculation against gas gangrene and all other immediate treatment, the cases are loaded straight on to an ambulance train, each C.C.S. having a siding to its own, in which a fully equipped and staffed train is always standing in readiness.

I and my own medical staff are responsible for all the arrangements as far back as the main dressing-station, right from the firing-line. I have introduced the system of working the motor ambulance on the cab-rank principle, i.e. each car as it returns from its last job goes into the rank like a taxi-cab, and as they are wanted the cars are taken in turn from the head of the rank, and the rest move up in turn.

During the battle of 12 October the work was very heavy. The average 'carry' from the front line was over 4,000 yards, through a heavy morass, and each stretcher took sixteen bearers, in four relays of four men in each – instead of two men as normally.

Throughout every department of the work, both fighting and feeding up supplies, stores and ammunition, I strive to introduce similar systematic methods and order, so that there shall be no muddling, no overlapping, no cross purposes, and everybody has to know exactly what his job is and when and where he has to do it. To carry this into effect one has to be very firm and very strict, and anybody who does not work up to time and come up to scratch usually does not get a second chance with me.

France, 8 November 1917.

To Miss Marjorie Barton,
    Addis Street, Perth, W.A.

Dear Miss Barton,
        Yesterday, upon opening a tin of Havelock tobacco, which was my personal share of a gift from the Australian Comforts Fund, I found a little slip of paper, with your name and address inside. I think you would like to receive a few lines from me, to convey to you my thanks for your share in this welcome gift, and to send you a message of greeting for Christmas. All we Australian men at the front appreciate most warmly all that our Australian womenfolk are doing for us, and the thought of all the girls we have left at home makes us very homesick. Can you realize what it is like for our boys not to have an Australian girl to talk to for months and months on end. I have myself the honour to command some 20,000 Australian boys, and, after three years of fighting, you may take it from me that they are the finest men in the world – brave, straight, devoted to duty, and ever ready to sacrifice themselves for their mates and their homeland. Also we have found out that our Australian girls are the finest girls in the world. We want no better.

                    With very kind regards,
                        John Monash.

France, 14 November 1917
The event long foreshadowed, and prompted by the

Commonwealth Government, has at last come to pass, and the C-in-C decided about ten days ago that all Australians should go into one corps. So from 1 January next the name Anzac will disappear from the corps, and '1st Anzac' will become 'The Australian Corps'. But the Chief is obdurate that the corps shall contain only four divisions, and as, at the same time, our reinforcements have fallen off so badly, it became a question as to which of the five divisions would have to go. It seems that the 4th Division is to go. They will not actually break it up, in case conscription goes through, and later we may be able to build it up again. But it goes away to the base and will be used as a recruiting ground for the other four divisions.

On 20 November Haig launched his last offensive of the year when General Byng's Third Army, using nearly 400 tanks, broke the German line at Cambrai, only to be forced back by enemy counter-attacks ten days later. By the end of 1917 the immense body and strength of the British Armies had been expended.

   Monash was appalled by the loss of life. 'I had formed the theory that the true role of infantry was not to expend itself upon heroic physical effort, nor to wither away under merciless machine-gun fire, nor to impale itself on hostile bayonets, nor to tear itself to pieces in hostile entanglements,' he later wrote, 'but, on the contrary to advance under the maximum possible protection of the maximum possible array of mechanical resources, in the form of guns, mortars and aeroplanes; to advance with as little impediment as possible; to be relieved as far as possible of the obligation to fight their way forward; to march, resolutely, regardless of the din and tumult of battle, to the appointed goal; and there to hold and defend the territory gained; and to gather in the form of prisoners, guns and stores, the fruits of victory.' Other generals had reached the same conclusion but had proved unable to achieve it. Monash was to show that this was possible.

III : VICTORY

Menton, 15 March, 1918
[An example of] Godley's *jeu d'esprit*. His corps, formerly 2nd Anzac, is now 22nd Corps. All corps and divisions have conventional signs to be used as marks on vehicles, baggage, billets, etc., in lieu of numbers, which latter would give away valuable information to spies. My sign is the swastika. [The old Runic sign, the swastika, was a popular symbol at the time: Rudyard Kipling used it as his personal mark on the spines and title pages of his books.] When Godley's corps received a new number it became a question of selecting a sign for the corps. Formations throughout France have all sorts of signs such as a black lion, a yellow horse shoe, a red and white chess-board, the red hand of Ulster, a leek, a red dragon, an eagle, an elephant, a viper, etc., animals predominating. Now in the *Tatler* there is published weekly 'A letter from Eve', and Eve is invariably, in all the quaint pictures of her, accompanied by her little dog 'Tou Tou' who is to be the conventional sign for Godley's corps.

I have occasionally mentioned my pierrot troupes. We have now brought them to a high state of excellence, and now have four troupes – one divisional one, and one for each infantry brigade. I have put in charge a thoroughly capable officer, with nothing else to do except to organize and manage these entertainments, which are of incalculable value to the troops. The principal company now has a full string orchestra of twenty-four performers under a highly capable conductor, Lance-Corporal Pierce, who can perform even Wagner very creditably. The company is now on a very high plane of merit. I hope you do not visualize a mere amateur show like at old-time camp-fire concerts. My troupes are real artists, and their performances are a high-class musical treat, staging operatic scenes, and putting on their numbers with full orchestral accompaniment and all the adjuncts of good scenery, lighting, and appropriate costumes. This divisional troupe includes two 'ladies', Lance-Corporal Watsford and Private Harvey, and I recently sent them to London to get a complete new outfit of wigs, gloves, shoes, hosiery, frocks, jewellery, etc., and the result is most startling. Both have beautiful clear soprano voices, and in the concerted numbers the combined effect of voice, bearing, and gesture is all that could be desired.

Menton, 16 March 1918

About that wristlet-watch of mine, your informant got the facts badly mixed up. The man who had my watch, Lance Corporal Garcia, did not (as you say) find it, but had it lent to him by me to use during a raid by my old 4th Brigade, while still under my command, at Bois Grenier on 2 July 1916. It was a luminous watch, and was needed by Garcia because he was the leader of a party whose movements had to be regulated by time. Garcia was badly wounded during this raid. Months afterwards he wrote me asking where he was to send the watch, and I replied saying I wished him to keep it as a souvenir of a brave deed ...

Menton, 24 March 1918

I intended to stay here another week, but have just half an hour ago received a telegram from Jess to say that my division had received orders to move up from the back area to the front. This is doubtless in consequence of the great Boche attack which commenced on 21 March.

The 'great Boche attack' of 21 March mentioned by Monash had been long expected, though none knew where or when it would fall. The fall of the Tsar a year earlier in March 1917 and the entry into the war of the United States in the following month had had little immediate effect on the course of the war, but the collapse of the Russian armies after the Bolshevik coup in November and the resulting armistice on the Eastern Front in February 1918 had enabled Ludendorff to transfer the bulk of his best divisions to the Western Front to deliver what he conceived as a knockout blow before the million-strong American army could take its place in the line. Ludendorff chose to strike his first hammerblow on the British Fifth Army front before Amiens, the key rail junction and meeting point of the British and French armies. The 'Kaiserbattle' began at dawn on 21 March 1918, the first day of the European spring, with a bombardment from 6,000 guns; forty-three German divisions fell on Gough's Fifth Army of seventeen divisions and shattered them. On 23 March, as the enemy tide surged

towards Amiens, Haig called on his last strong reserve, the Aus-
tralian Corps, to 'plug the gap' before Amiens, and Birdwood
ordered his divisions south with the words: 'Boys, I know that
I can confidently appeal to every single individual in the AIF
to "take the strain" for the sake of his country and all he holds
dear.'

France, 2 April 1918

I seize upon a little interlude of comparative leisure to
try and give you a connected account of the very exciting events of the past few days. When the great German
offensive broke out on 21 March, I was at Menton,
intending to remain there until the end of the month.
One of my brigadiers, Brigadier-General Rosenthal,
had also come down a day or two before on sick leave,
really to recoup after having been slightly gassed, and
was staying at Lord Michelin's home for convalescent
officers at Cap Martin close to Menton. He and I spent
the whole of Saturday the 23rd together in making a
very pleasant mountain tour to La Turbie. We had separated for the day and had planned to make up a motor
party next day to go into Italy as far as San Remo. The
newspapers that evening gave us the first news of what
was happening, and I felt that it was inevitable that we
ought to return at once. I had left my division in a back
area (Nielles-les-Blequin) about twenty miles east of
Boulogne, resting and training, and I was convinced that
it would only be a matter of days before they would be
drawn into the fight in some capacity or other. While I
was deliberating what I had better do, a telegram arrived
from Jess to say that the division had been ordered to

move eastward towards Ypres, and although I could not quite understand why the move should be in that direction, the news made me decide definitely to return the next day. By dint of my rank I got the authorities at Cap Martin to make special arrangements to reserve a carriage on the train on Sunday morning, 24 March, for myself and General Rosenthal, and I wired to Jess to send Paul with my car to Paris. The train arrived at 8.45 on Monday morning 25th. It was on Sunday the 24th that Paris was heavily shelled for the first time by that wonderful long range gun.

As regards my description of what follows, I am enclosing herewith a piece of a map showing the area in which I became interested and most of the places which I now mention you will find with a little searching on that map.

Paul [Simonson] duly met me at the Gare de Lyon with the car and we stayed in Paris only long enough to get a snatch of breakfast and a wash and to pick up some baggage which I had left there on my way down south. By ten o'clock we were clear of Paris and bowling at a great rate along splendid roads via Beauvais to Amiens. At Amiens we found everything in a state of frightful confusion. The Boche had been heavily bombing the town and civilians were evacuating it rapidly. There was great excitement. The railway square and the streets were full of war-worn, mud-spattered, excited, and starved-looking troops of all kinds, and excited officers and other ranks who had been on leave and were struggling to get back to their units in various parts of the front. At Amiens, which is an important interchange

station, all the normal activities of the city seemed to
have been arrested. The railway transport officers and
the military authorities in the town had no news of the
events at the front, had been working for several days
with their staff without sleep, and were in a condition
almost of mental paralysis. The ordinary supply-depots
had ceased to function; we could hardly get any petrol,
and it was with some difficulty we managed to get some
lunch. At the railway station I was fortunate enough to
pick up letters from Jess which Wieck had brought
down that morning, telling me that the division on its
march towards Ypres had been intercepted on the road
and deflected southward, that it would lie that night at
Blaringhem (just north of the map). And that it had
been ordered to stand by to entrain during that night
and next day for Doullens. Wieck had come down
ahead to try and find the 10th Corps headquarters, as it
was understood that we should report to the 10th Corps
for orders.

I thereupon decided to push on to Doullens to get
closer and more definite news. Arrived there about
three o'clock and found a motor-omnibus load of my
officers and N.C.Os just arrived, they having been sent
down from the division to stand by for billeting duties
when it had been determined where the division was to
go. There I got into touch with Captain Pyke and
Major Wieck, who were out examining the various villages in the vicinity for billeting accommodation but
had no further news. At Doullens there was still greater
confusion and streams of soldier stragglers pouring in
from the east with the most hair-raising stories, that the

Boche was almost on top of them. Viewed from that particular locality it almost looked as if the whole British Army in this part of the world was in a state of rout. As it was impossible to find anybody in authority who knew anything of value, I decided again to push on and get in touch with my own headquarters. This I did, reaching Blaringhem at about seven o'clock and found there everything packed up to be ready for a shift next day. All that night my infantry were entraining at three stations, respectively Arques, St Omer, and Steenbecque. The artillery and divisional ammunition column were already on the march southwards.

I snatched a few hours' sleep at Blaringhem and left early on the morning of 26 March for the south, trying to find the 10th Corps. By this time of course, the trouble was that all headquarters, divisional corps, and army, were rapidly on the move backwards and did not remain more than a few hours in any one town. All signal communication by telephone or telegraph was of course cut off, and, as the whole place was full of the wildest and most contradictory rumours, it was very difficult to locate anybody.

However, I managed to glean that 10th Corps was moving to Hautecloque (north-west corner of the map), and reaching there learned that the corps commander of the 10th Corps was still at Frévent. There I repaired with all haste and learned from him that he was trying to collect a few divisions with a view to making a stand east of Doullens, and generally re-establish a line between Arras and Albert. He could give me no definite orders, except to concentrate my division to the east of

Doullens and there await further orders.

We pushed onto Doullens, and there tumbled into a scene of almost indescribable confusion. During the twenty-four hours between my two visits to that town there had been a great change in the atmosphere. Doullens was full of civilian refugees and many thousands of soldiers who had got detached from their units and were streaming in from the east. All had the wildest stories and all looked starved and broken down with fatigue and want of sleep. There must have been a great conference between the British and French High Command in the Mairie at Doullens, for the town square was packed full of motor cars and brilliantly uniformed French and British officers.

Here occurred another piece of good fortune on a par with all that seems to have dogged my footsteps throughout all these exciting times. I arrived at Doullens railway station just at the very moment that the first train bringing some of the troops of my 9th Brigade arrived ... [with] Headquarters [and] Brigadier-General Rosenthal and all his staff and signal personnel, etc., and a portion of the 33rd Battalion. While they were in the act of detraining, an excited officer, who proved to be the Town Major of Doullens, rushed up to say that a report had just come in that a number of German armoured motor cars had broken through at Hébuterne, and that the German cavalry were within ten miles of the town. (I may say that these rumours were subsequently proved to be without foundation.)

I instructed General Rosenthal at once to collect all the troops he could and temporarily take up a position to cover Doullens, so that my detrainment at that station from the numerous trains subsequently to arrive might be carried out without interference. Knowing that my 10th Brigade was to detrain at Mondicourt, Paul and I motored as fast as possible to that town and again I arrived just as General McNicoll's first train drew into the station. We rapidly got all the troops out and McNicoll took up with a portion of the 37th Battalion a position to cover the detrainment at Mondicourt. All the roads leading from the south-east into Mondicourt were simply packed with wild-eyed Tommies, refugees on foot and in every conceivable conveyance with their furniture and wheelbarrows, hand-carts, farm-wagons, and the like, and every conceivable kind of military vehicle streaming north-west. Everybody interrogated appeared to have the idea that the Boche was just behind him on his very heels. I put on military police to establish straggler-posts and we held up hundreds of Tommies with and without rifles and equipment, and formed them into bodies suitable for employment if required. I proceeded myself to Couturelle (just north of Dullens-Arras Road) and selected a chateau for my headquarters and established signal communications with the 10th Corps at Frévent. There I learned that there was no confirmation of the report that the Boche motor cars had broken through at Hébuterne. I also learned that General Maclagan had arrived at Basseux (in the direction of Arras) and that the 4th Australian Division was in the act of arriving in the area. I drove at once by car to Basseux and got into touch with Macla-gan. He told me that he had only one brigade of

infantry in hand and had sent them in the direction of
Hébuterne to close what was evidently a gap in the
British line. This brigade was my old 4th Brigade under
General Brand. I then rushed back to Mondicourt as
quickly as the congested state of the road would allow.
Every kind of vehicle in every stage of panic was in train
along this road towards Doullens, and that the enemy
was not far away was evidenced by the fact that numerous shells fell on and near the road as we passed,
scattering the traffic in all directions. It was really amusing to see the Tommy transport galloping wildly all over
the adjacent fields. Much of this panic proved to be
quite without justification.

Again reaching Mondicourt, I there issued orders
for the concentration of my three brigades – 9th
Brigade at Pas, 10th at Authie, and 11th at Coiun,
although up to that time none of the units of the 11th
Brigade had yet arrived by train. I then returned by car
to my chateau at Couturelle reaching there about 8 p.m.
A dispatch rider arrived from the 10th Corps, to say that
the 10th Corps was no longer G.H.Q. Reserve but had
passed under the command of the Third Army (General
Byng). He was followed within about an hour by a
second dispatch rider with orders that I should personally report at once to the 7th Corps at Corbie, as orders
had been received that the division would probably be
transferred to the 7th Corps and act under its orders. I
was getting ready to proceed there, when a further dispatch rider arrived stating that the 7th Corps had had to
abandon Corbie, as it was being heavily shelled, and
were transferring to Montigny. I felt sure that the situa-

tion was critical and that energetic action would be necessary, so I decided to take with me in addition to Paul an officer of my general staff , an officer of my administrative staff, my D.A.D.M.S., and the officer commanding divisional signals , also two dispatch riders on motor-bicycles.

We left Mondicourt about 10 p.m. and I made the best of my way to Montigny. Luckily it was a moonlight night but the roads were fearfully congested with refugee traffic, swarms of soldiers pouring westward and thousands of motor-lorries, heavy guns and all kinds of military vehicles. Our progress was painfully slow, and it was one o'clock in the morning before I reached Montigny, and I had considerable difficulty in locating the chateau in which Lieutenant-General Congreve, commander of the 7th Corps, was in the act of taking up his quarters. I found that the whole headquarters (comprising a total personnel of about 500) had cleared out of Corbie in the late afternoon in a great hurry, abandoning most of their papers and kit, and found them sitting very disconsolately in a dark building, practically wringing their hands, as all the divisions of the corps had been biffed badly that day. The only men in the crowd who seemed to have their wits about them were the corps commander, Lieutenant-General Congreve, and his B.G.G.S. (Chief staff officer), Hore-Ruthven (whom you will doubtless remember as one of the A.D.Cs to Lord Brassey). Both these men are V.Cs. They were seated at a little table with their maps spread in front of them, examining them by the light of a flickering candle. As I stepped into the room General Congreve said – 'Thank heaven, the Australians at last.' Our conversation was of the briefest. He said – 'General, the position is very simple. My corps at four o'clock today was holding the line from Bray to Albert, when the line broke, and what is left of the three divisions in the line after four days' heavy fighting without food or sleep are falling back rapidly. German cavalry have been seen approaching Morlancourt and Buire. They are making straight for Amiens. What I want you to do is to get into the angle between the Ancre and the Somme as far east as possible and stop him.'

This constituted the whole of my orders. I got them to place a small room at my disposal and give me the use of a telephone and from there worked all night to make the necessary arrangements. Ringing up General Byng, I got Third Army to arrange for motor buses to bring down my infantry as quickly as possible, telegraphing Jess at Couturelle what to do. I then prepared the whole of my orders for my dispositions, and dispatched my staff officers in various directions to make the necessary arrangements. I sent Paul back with my car to Couturelle to bring along my batman and the rest of my baggage. I got practically no sleep that night.

Shortly after daybreak Paul arrived with some more staff officers and my baggage, and we proceeded to Franvillers, around which on the map I have drawn a red circle. It was from this town that I directed operations for the first few hours. From the high ground at Franvillers we could plainly see the German cavalry operating on the high ground to the south of Morlancourt. It was really a question of an hour one way or the other whether we could intercept him or not. I did not know how long it would take any of my infantry to arrive.

You can imagine my relief when the first bus convoy arrived from the north into Franvillers bringing General Cannan and two battalions of the 11th Brigade. This convoy consisted of sixty motor buses, old London motor-bus type, all crowded with troops, fully armed and with plenty of ammunition. It was a miracle of good management. Without a moment's delay we marched them off along the road to Heilly and they deployed rapidly along the line from Mericourt to Sailly-le-Sec, which I have marked on the map with a red line.

At ten o'clock the first two battalions of the 10th Brigade arrived (also by bus) together with General McNicoll, and an hour afterwards some of the 9th Brigade with General Rosenthal. By two o'clock I already had over 5,000 troops under my hands, and these were all rapidly disposed across the ridge in the angle between the Ancre and the Somme during the afternoon, sending out patrols to get into contact with the enemy.

With the exception of desultory shelling of the various villages in the neighbourhood the enemy showed no great activity, as he soon discovered that there were troops blocking his path, and he evidently pulled up his rush in a spirit of caution to enable him to test our strength.

During that day (27 March) and the following night the remainder of my infantry arrived by train at Doullens and embussed direct to Franvillers, and my two brigades of artillery with divisional ammunition column, pioneer battalion, and many other units were well on the way route marching. By the early morning of 28 March I had the greater part of my division billeted in the villages of Ribemont, Heilly, Franvillers, and Lahoussoye.

From that time onward the position I had taken up grew hourly stronger, and during the day of the 28th two more of Maclagan's brigades arrived and took up positions respectively west of Albert and south-east of Lavieville. The tired and beaten troops of the 35th, 21st and 9th Divisions, now reduced to a mere handful, took up a rough line along the railway between Mericourt and Albert. We also heard that the New Zealand Division had got forward further north and that the 2nd Canadians were between them and Arras.

We thus had a sprinkling of stout first-class divisions at various parts of the line, and the effect of their arrival was electric and remarkable. The advent of my own division at the place marked had an astonishing effect in stiffening up everybody on both flanks, and the tendency to run was checked; people began to regain confidence, and measures for reorganization of the whole line were rapidly commenced. During the night of 28 March I pushed my line out 2,000 yards eastward until they were in actual contact with enemy patrols. In the afternoon the expected happened, and he attacked me in considerable force – the 3rd German Naval Division on the right or north, the 13th Prussian Division in the centre, and the 18th Schleswig-Holstein Division on the left or south. Overnight I had got all my artillery into position behind my line and the battle was a walk-over for us. We simply slaughtered the enemy wholesale, both with machine-gun fire and with artillery. After an hour the whole attack had petered out, and this up to the time of writing is the end of the German attempt to capture Amiens by direct approach. We captured prisoners from all three divisions opposite us; one of them carried an autographed photo of the divisional commander (General-Major Bloch von Blottwitz). This photograph I have sent you under separate cover. It is rather interesting that I heard today from another prisoner that this divisional commander had been killed during this battle by a direct hit from one of Grimwade's shells.

Most of the villages in the neighbourhood had of course been hurriedly evacuated by the inhabitants, and I have been at great pains to try and have gathered up all the fowls, pigs, cattle and sheep and have had them driven back to concentration camps. I quickly had all the villages policed with good stout Australians and we rapidly restored order.

On the night of 29 March General Maclagan's troops came into the line on my immediate left and had several brushes with the enemy which were all in our favour. The 5th Australian Division meanwhile also arrived and came in north of Maclagan, linking up with the New Zealanders, so that we now present a strong united front over a frontage of some twelve miles and the enemy will batter himself against it in vain.

The main disaster to the British Front in this part arose through the failure of the Fifth Army, which held

the line south of the Somme. Fifth Army has been practically pulverized into fragments and its commander
(General Gough) has been sent home. The French
immediately took over the defence of the line south of
the Somme, but have moved slowly and for several days
the situation on my right flank was very obscure. I
therefore made all preparations to defend the line of the
Somme west of Sailly-le-Sec as far as Aubigny in case
the enemy tried to get behind me, but since yesterday
the position down south is much more satisfactory, as I
sent Rosenthal with the 9th Brigade to Cachy, and the
mere presence of this brigade in that locality seemed to
stiffen up everybody still forward.

From conversation with German prisoners I
learned that they had had no idea that the Australians
were in this part of the world. Our press correspondents
are forbidden even to mention the fact that Australians
are in this vicinity, and several long cables which I know
are ready to go to Australia have been held up in consequence. The full story, therefore, of what Australians and
New Zealanders have done to entirely retrieve the situation will probably not be known to the world at large
until the news has become stale.

As Franvillers was in full view of the enemy and
began to come under shell-fire, I yesterday shifted my
headquarters back to St Gratien, where I am inhabiting
a very fine Louis XI chateau belonging to the Comte de
Thielloye, who has made us very comfortable. I also
received the good news that the 2nd Australian Division
is on the way down and will detrain to-morrow at
Amiens, and the 1st Australian Division is soon to

follow. I expect it will not be many days before our own corps headquarters also arrives and we shall again be a united family. We are highly elated with our successes and have received the most flattering congratulations.

3rd Aust. Div. Headquarters,
France, 3 April 1918

Dr Felix Meyer,
    Melbourne

My dear Felix,

I often have to carry on my heavy correspondence, official and personal, in the short intervals between stirring events ... The purpose of this letter really is to thank you most warmly for your kind congratulations on my knighthood. I observe with some interest from the tone of yours and letters from many others that my friends in Australia seem to regard it as recompense to me personally for patriotic services. From this point of view a Knighthood of the Bath would be a reward far beyond my deserts. It is really, however, a distinction to the magnificent division of which it has been my good fortune to be placed in command, in recognition of the series of brilliant victories achieved by the divisions during the spring, summer, and autumn campaigns of 1917. To exercise the command of such a division, and of such men, is an honour far greater than can be accorded by the grant of any titles. The troops consist of the very flower of our Australian youth. From every point of view they are magnificent. The officers (the

great majority of whom I have promoted from the
ranks) represent the cream of our professional and educated classes, young engineers, architects, medicals,
accountants, pastoralists, public-school boys and so on.
For the first twelve months after the assembly in England and France of this fine body of men as a division,
they slaved unremittingly under such guidance as I was
able to give them to learn the art of war in its many
branches; and for the past twelve months they have
fought as veterans, with never a failure, and with a cor-
porate spirit and a collective functioning which has
made of the 3rd Australian Division one of the crack
divisions in France ...

Yours very sincerely,
John Monash

France, 23 April 1918

Since the heavy fighting in the first week of this month
to establish our firm grip upon the plateau between the
Somme and the Ancre, the enemy has shown no dispo-
sition to attack. This monotony was suddenly relieved
this morning by an event of highly dramatic interest.

You will doubtless long ago have heard of the
famous German airman, Richthofen, the most successful and most brilliant of all the German fliers. He was
himself a Flight Commander and commanded No. 11
Pursuit Flight or 'Jagdstaffel', which was always easily
recognized by the fact that all the fuselages of these
machines were painted a bright vermilion. You could
always tell when Richthofen was about by these red
machines, and their appearance in the air was always

promptly noted and reported.

Richthofen's full name was Rittmeister Freiherr Manfred von Richthofen, he having been a cavalry captain before joining the German Flying Corps. In the German *communiques* of 22 April, it was claimed for him that he had on the day before brought down his seventy-ninth and eightieth victims. He was engaged in attempting to bring down his eighty-first victim when he himself met his end.

The whole drama took place immediately over my 11th Brigade headquarters, near which were also several artillery batteries. The brigade headquarters itself and all these batteries have anti-aircraft defences, manned by Lewis-guns with special sighting attachments, and the Lewis-gunners are always very keen to get into action against low-fling enemy aeroplanes. After the event of this morning they will be keener than ever.

Richthofen's flight was seen travelling at a considerable height overhead, probably 7,000 feet, and engaged a formation of our own machines consisting of R.E.8s. Some fighting took place in the air, and then suddenly one of our R.E.8s made a quick dive to within 150 feet of the ground, followed by Richthofen in a fast triplane, which rapidly overhauled our machine, and we could see him pumping tracer bullets after our machine. All the Lewis-gunners in the neighbourhood immediately opened fire and made an awful row. Suddenly Richfhofen's machine was seen to stagger, but recovered itself and made as if to fly off. In turning it flew directly over one of General Hobb's batteries in the vicinity, whose Lewis-gun was manned by the battery cook and his assistant cook. A lucky stream of bullets got the machine fair and square; it turned over, came down with a crash, and was completely wrecked.

Before the machine could be approached the enemy artillery, which, like us, had seen the aeroplane come down and had marked the spot, put down a circle of shrapnel all around it and maintained their fire for about half an hour, while Richthofen's Flight circled round overhead four or five times and then majestically flew away. Such was the requiem of this doughty and chivalrous warrior. When our people could get near the aeroplane they found that Richthofen had been shot through the head and heart by bullets and the papers on the body left no doubt as to his identity.

Our Royal Air Force was soon on the ground; the wrecked machine and the body of Richthofen were brought in, and late in the day buried with military honours. His personal effects were afterwards taken over the German lines and dropped with a message of condolence from the Royal Air Force.

Baron Manfred von Richthofen − known as the 'Red Baron' from his red-painted Albatross fighter, which was superior until 1918 to any British aircraft − was the greatest German 'ace' and a national hero in Germany; a chivalrous but deadly opponent, he was a legendary figure even to his enemies. Canadians insist that one of their pilots, chasing the Red Baron, fired the bursts that killed him but Australians demur. One of von Richthofen's pilots in his 'Flying Circus' was Hermann Goering, later Hitler's Luftwaffe leader.

France, 26 April 1918

Anzac Day was celebrated yesterday with sheafs of telegrams sent and received between all old Gallipoli men who took part in the fighting. The day was also signalized by a wonderful fight carried out by the 13th and 15th Australian Brigades (Glasgow and Elliott), both of which brigades have been under my orders for the past few weeks. My 9th Brigade had securely kept the Boche out of the town of Villers-Bretonneux for three weeks. They were then withdrawn for a rest on 23 April and the 8th British Division (regulars) took over the town from them. On 24 April the Boche attacked (with four divisions) and took the town. Late at night we had to organize a counter-attack. This was undertaken by the 13th and 15th Brigades in the early hours of Anzac Day. They advanced 3,000 yards in the dark without artillery support, completely restored the position, and captured over 1000 prisoners. I can see the prisoners pouring past this chateau from the window of my office as I write this letter. It was a magnificent performance.

'Villers-Bret', the town defended by Australians during the March crisis and then recaptured by them in this brilliant night action, became after the war the site of Australia's national war cemetery in France.

France, 2 May 1918

I enclose herewith a tiny piece of the red fabric off Richthofen's aeroplane, the 'Red Falcon', in which he was brought down by us. I also have a piece of the wooden propeller from the same machine. Last night we brought down another plane quite near my chateau. The pilot was slightly wounded, but the officer-observer was quite all right. He was brought in to me; I gave him a glass of wine, and he talked freely. He told me that the German Flieger Corps much appreciated the action of our No. 3 Australian Flying Squadron in placing a wreath on Richthofen's grave.

I enclose also cutting from a French daily paper – 'The Australians cover themselves with glory.' You can hardly picture the delight of the French population during the three weeks when the 150,000 Australians arrived on this front to cover Amiens. The knew it meant for them safety and a retention of their homes and property. It was the same story when the 1st Australian Division was sent hastily back to Flanders and stopped the Boche advance west of Bailleul …

Here is also the *Daily Telegraph* account of our recapture of Villers-Bretonneux by the 13th and 15th Brigades. In my opinion this counter-attack at night, without artillery support, is the finest thing yet done in the war by Australians or any other troops. Philip Gibbs's article is the first public avowal of this brilliant episode which took place in the early hours of Anzac Day. The total prisoners taken finally exceeded 900. The British public is at last beginning to sit up and take notice, and from an attitude of cold and rather critical patronage towards Australians, and vague allusion to their 'slack discipline' (forsooth), the people in England, the English troops and officers, and finally the War Office itself, are beginning to realize that the Australians are some of the best troops in the whole Empire, always to be relied upon, not merely to hold securely all ground but also to carry out every reasonable task set them.

France, 7 May 1918

The night before last the division had another brilliant success about which you will doubtless have heard by cable long before now. Seizing a sudden opportunity of a change in an enemy division opposite to me, I made arrangements for a surprise attack. This was carried out by Rosenthal's brigade and was completely successful. We captured 200 prisoners and fifteen machine-guns, and advanced our line half a mile over a frontage of one and a half miles, or a greater gain of ground than at Messines.

In reply to your questions: Undue familiarity between the various grades is strongly discouraged. The various ranks keep to themselves both on and off duty, but the officer has to look after the comfort and well-being of his men and animals first, before he thinks of food and rest for himself, and further he must share all their dangers and hardships. This is the true road to ensuing their loyal service and obedience to his orders ...

France, 14 May 1918

I expect within a few days to be appointed to the command of the Australian Army Corps, in place of General Birdwood, who will be appointed to the command of a new army of which this corps will probably in the near future form part. This appointment will carry with it my promotion to the rank of lieutenant-general.

The Australian Corps is much the largest of any of the twenty army corps in France, for it contains all the five Australian divisions ... Moreover owing to the great prestige won by the corps during the last three months, it is much the finest corps command in the British Army ...

Monash's appointment as commander of the Australian Corps seems inevitable, his promotion smooth; but it was not so. Haig had profound confidence in Monash and so did Birdwood, and both men believed that the time had come when the Australians should be commanded by one of their own generals, as the Canadian Corps had been since July 1917. When Birdwood was offered command of the reconstituted 5th Army, while retaining command of the AIF as a whole, he recommended Monash as his successor as Corps Commander and Hughes approved his recommendation on 18 May 1918. Charles Bean was disturbed by this. An unreserved admirer of Brudenell White, whom he saw as the finest type of 'Britisher' and the natural successor to Birdwood, he left France the same day for London to conspire with Keith Murdoch to thwart Monash's promotion, embarking on a convoluted series of personal discussions with Hughes, General Wilson, the CIGS, and even Lloyd George, in attempts to discredit Monash. When Birdwood and White refused to be party to the intrigue, Monash's appointment was announced, effective 1 June. Bean later had the grace to admit he had been wrong in his judgement of Monash, and wrote in his volume covering the events of 1918: 'From the time of Monash's advent the corps had at its head a very great mind — certainly one of the greatest that has ever controlled a British military force.'

Monash's new staff welcomed the change. Among them was the Chief of Staff, Brigadier-General Thomas Blamey, Australia's future field-marshal. 'He possessed a mind cultured far above the average, widely informed, alert and prehensile,' Monash wrote of Blamey. 'He served me with exemplary loyalty, for which I owe him a debt of gratitude which cannot be repaid.' Blamey repaid this liking. Monash's command of the corps differed from Birdwood's. 'Birdie', who hated being at his desk and left paperwork to his patient Chief of Staff, General White, was (according to Monash in later years) 'always "buzzing about", looking people up, perambulating all over the place, hardly ever at his headquarters'. Monash spent all his time at his HQ, 'considering reports, planning, organizing, and directing'. F.M. Cutlack, who was his divisional intelligence officer in 1917, wrote of the 'Old Man', as his staff called him: 'Without interfering with their work he insisted upon knowing every detail of the organization under his command in all operations; the work of the machine fascinated him and its efficiency was a passion with him.'

France, 26 May 1918
[To a little girl]

My dear Susan,

In France here the weather has been very warm, and this has brought [out] all the beautiful wild flowers. The other day we took prisoner a beautiful German messenger dog. He is a beautiful Alsatian wolf-hound, and is very friendly. He has learned to understand English, and is very faithful to us, and we all pet him ...

Aus. Corps H.Q., France,
31 May 1918

As foreshadowed in my letter of 14 May I have today
taken over command of the Australian Army Corps. My
promotion has already been definitely approved by the
Army Council and the Commonwealth Government,
and it is only a matter of a few days when it will be
formally announced in orders. My new command comprises a total at present of 166,000 troops, and covers
practically the whole Australian field army in France.
My jurisdiction does not extend to England and the
depots, nor to certain stationary hospitals and small base
units in France, which latter are nominally under direct
army control. But for all practical purposes I am now
the supreme Australian commander, and thus at long last
the Australian nation has achieved its ambition of having
its own Commander-in-Chief, a native born Australian
– for the first time in its history.

My command is more than two and a half times
the size of the British Army under the Duke of Wellington, or of the French Army under Napoleon Bonaparte,
at the battle of Waterloo. Moreover I have in the Army
Corps an artillery which is more than six times as
numerous and more than a hundred times as powerful
as that commanded by the Duke of Wellington. I have
besides arms services and departments not dreamt of in
his day, all of the highest scientific complexity.

I shall in due course, in the hope that it will interest you, have compiled and send you a complete list of
all the units and troops which compose the Army
Corps. The chief elements are, of course, the five divi-

sions each commanded by a major-general, and in addition nearly 70,000 corps troops ...

France, 8 June 1918

You will notice that I have in the corps 1,000 American
engineers. Of the total troops of the corps, something
like 50,000 are not Australians, and of those 50,000
about 25,000 are British regulars, the balance being 'new
army'. Among the artillery you will find two Royal
Horse Artillery brigades.

I am pleased to say that my flying squadron is
wholly Australian and is one of the most efficient
squadrons in France. Its twenty aeroplanes do all my air
reconnaisances, photography, and counter-battery rang-
ing. The heavy artillery is roughly divided into siege
artillery, which does bombardment work, and heavy
artillery, which does counter-battery work, although
there is no very strict line of demarcation between
the two. Some of the larger guns have ranges up to
20,000 yards, and I am shortly getting two 12-inch
high-velocity guns having a range of over 32,000 yards.
These latter guns are on railway mountings, and the
gun, with its carriage and railway truck on sixteen axles,
weighs complete 192 tons. It can of course only be used
from a railway, and after doing its firing it is hauled away
to a safe place in rear. With these guns we engage distant enemy railway stations and railway junctions, so as
to interfere with the enemy communications.

France, 18 June 1918

Last week I held my first Divisional Commanders'

Conference, which was attended by all the major-generals and their chiefs of staff. At the conclusion of the proceedings, Major-General Sir Talbot Hobbs drew attention to the extreme historical significance of this meeting; it being the first occasion in the history of Australia that such a Council of War had been held, in the very middle of a great campaign and close up to the front, where every member present was a native-born Australian. This is an episode which might very well be made widely known in Australia and one of which the Australian nation has every reason to be very proud.

France, 25 June 1918

In a recent letter I forward you a copy of a letter from London. An intrigue going on is taking all sorts of subtle forms. Certain people strongly desire to displace Birdwood. They fear the Australian public would resent his being got rid of, so they have already started propaganda to make it appear that he will be too busy as an army commander to attend to AIF work. They know, of course, that B. cannot be got rid of unless another man, equally acceptable to the War Office, the AIF, and the Australian Government can be found. No such man can be found other than myself. In order to induce me to accept such a position, they propose to try and win me with the offer of further promotion and, of course, increased status and emoluments. As they fear that I would decline these temptations, and as the only excuse for getting rid of B. is that they wish to separate the functions of corps commander from those of G.O.C., A.I.F., their first problem is to displace me from the corps. In order to bring this about they have started an attempt to attack my capacity to command the corps, and are putting about propaganda that Brudenell White, being a permanent soldier, would be better fitted for this job, and that it would be in Australia's best future interests that he should get the appointment. These proceedings are being undertaken in London, in order to bring pressure to bear upon Mr Hughes.

My own personal view is that I cannot relinquish the corps command until I have made a proved success of it without impairing my prestige and, further, without a certain amount of infidelity to B. I propose, therefore, to fight them on their own ground and to insist upon retaining the command of the corps. In this battle I possess of course very many and very strong cards, and some of them are trump cards, among which is my undoubted belief that both Rawlinson and the Chief will see me through.

I daresay the Australian public are entirely innocent and ignorant of all that is going on, and, quite evidently, the Australian Government, as represented by Watt and Pearce, have so far not been influenced by the matter.

I write in detail on this matter to you because there is, of course, no telling what may happen in the near future, and if you know what is in the wind you may be able to understand better any future developments that may appear in the Australian press.

In the words of his biographer, Geoffrey Serle, 'Monash's greatest claim to military fame may lie in the model example he gave at Hamel of the concerted use of infantry, artillery, tanks and aircraft and its subsequent application by the British Army'.

Early in June 1918, as the Australians carried out their private summer war, an incessant nibbling of the German lines they called 'peaceful penetration', Monash and his divisional commanders discussed a limited offensive against the German salient, specifically the capture of Hamel. The arrival in the Fourth Army of the remarkable Mark V tank was the deciding factor. It was heavily armoured, capable of traversing level ground at 10 kph, and carried a 6-pounder gun. On 21 June Monash submitted to Rawlinson a plan to seize Hamel with a pre-dawn attack by four brigades, preceded by an intense artillery bombardment and assisted by tanks. The tanks would be directed by the infantry in overcoming strongpoints and would be re-supplied with ammunition by four carrier tanks and by air drops.

The capture of Hamel began at 3.02 a.m. 4 July 1918, with an artillery bombardment which effectively drowned the noise of the assembling tanks; eight minutes later the main bombardment fell on the enemy lines and the infantry went forward, following a creeping barrage that shifted forward every four minutes, tanks following the infantry. It was all over in 93 minutes, for a cost of 1,400 casualties (German losses in killed, wounded and captured were twice as heavy). 'It wasn't a battle at all – just a Sunday morning stroll,' one soldier commented. None of the tanks was lost and only three were disabled. It was a short, sharp, brilliant victory. Monash's battle plans were circulated widely among British divisional commanders as models of clarity.

France, 5 July 1918

The three events of greatest importance since last I wrote, are the battle of Hamel and the visits of the Commander-in-Chief and of the [Australian] Prime Minister and Mr Cook. I have time only to allude to these interesting events in the briefest detail.

The Chief [Field-Marshal Haig] came to see me on 2 July, spending over an hour with me talking over my plans for the capture of Hamel. He himself had to rush away to the Versailles Conference, but his chief artillery commander, Birch, stayed to lunch. As ever Sir Douglas was affability, courtesy, and consideration personified. He always expresses the very greatest confidence in me.

On 3 July, although it proved a most highly inconvenient day, I received a long visit from [the Australian Prime Minister] Mr Hughes, Mr Joseph Cook, with their staff and two journalists (Murdoch and Gilmour). They made a tour lasting from ten o'clock in the morning to seven in the evening around the corps area travelling hard all the time and giving Mr Hughes an opportunity of addressing bodies of troops. He saw about 5 per cent of the whole command and the arrangements all worked like clockwork, and he left the same evening for Paris highly pleased. He formally tendered to me the thanks of the Commonwealth Government, and spoke most charmingly.

On 4 July I carried out the battle for the capture of Hamel, which, as cabled, was a brilliant success. No fighting operation that the corps has ever undertaken has been more brilliantly, cleanly and perfectly carried

through, without the slightest hitch. You will have
learned all about it from the papers long before now.
I send you herewith the original telegrams of congratulations received from the Prime Minister, the
Commander-in-Chief, and the Army Commander.

France, 10 July 1918

The principal event of the past week was the visit by
M. Clemenceau, the Prime Minister of France, an old
man seventy-eight years of age, who came specially from
Paris to congratulate the Australians. I took him towards
the front and collected a body of the battle troops (4th,
6th and 11th Brigades) and he made to them a very fine
and fiery oration, in very good English. I have had a
number of photographs taken of the occasion, some in
colour, and shall try and get copies to send you.

France, 2 August 1918

I am now in the middle of preparations for a very large
battle. It will employ the whole resources of my corps
command, including the 1st Australian Division which
commences to arrive in my corps area in two days' time.
Mine will not be the only corps employed and if successful it will be a very big show indeed. I shall send you
the latest particulars as time permits later, but I am sure
you can quite realize how extremely busy I am and what
an enormous undertaking I have in hand, to plan a
battle on such a large scale and to co-ordinate the
actions of so many people. These brief references to
these events must suffice for the present.

*The 'very big show indeed' Monash mentions was the forth-
coming offensive by the Australian and Canadian Corps from
Villers-Bretonneux east of Amiens on 8 August 1918, a battle
of which he was principal architect.*

*Success has many fathers and Monash never claimed the
entire credit for its planning, but no one had more to do than
he with its origination and successful execution. His steady
hand can be seen in its every aspect.*

*As early as 23 May Haig had suggested to Rawlinson,
commanding the Fourth Army, that he consider an offensive
using the Australians and Canadians, but planning lapsed
when the great German offensive against the French front
began on 27 May. The stunning capture of Hamel on 4 July
and Mangin's successful French counter-offensive against the
Siossons salient on 18 July indicated that the enemy was seriously over-extended and the quality of his troops deteriorating.
The German salient east of Amiens could perhaps also be elim-
inated. Since 4 July Monash had seen Rawlinson and his
Chief of Staff, Archibald Montgomery, practically every day,
and had proposed mounting an offensive, while asking for the
return of 1st Division and the involvement of the Canadian
Corps. On 21 July Rawlinson asked Monash and his Canadian counterpart, Currie, to work on a plan of attack
employing both Corps, 'and gave them a free hand on tactics'
(in Geoffrey Serle's words). Monash planned a deep penetration, one deep enough to capture the enemy gun line and
prevent retaliatory bombardment. Forwarding his plans to
Haig, he snatched a few days' leave in London, receiving an
urgent summons to return on 29 July. Marshal Foch had given
his assent to the operation on 24 July. On 31 July Monash
assembled his divisional commanders, telling Haig, who*

attended the meeting, that he was delighted to be recalled from
leave and that he had 'all the threads of the operations in his
hands'. He asked for tanks, nearly 500 of them, and aircraft for
reconnaissance and air supply, nearly 800 of them. His artillery
would number 2,000 guns. The enemy suspected nothing, and
were unaware even of the arrival of the Canadian Corps on the
Amiens front under conditions of great secrecy.

Rawlinson would use three corps, the Canadians and
Australians south of the Somme, British III Corps north of the
river, and ordered a three-stage advance on the day – 'the first
under a creeping barrage, the second supported by mobile
artillery and tanks, and the third a period of exploitation'
(in Geoffrey Serle's words). It was hoped to penetrate nine
to sixteen kilometres. Australian Corps would attack on a
seven-kilometre front with brigades from 2nd and 3rd Divisions, brigades from 4th and 5th Divisions taking over from
them for Phases 2 and 3 – 'leap-frogging' – with a tank allo-
cated to each infantry company. (1st Division would form corps
reserve.)

On the day before the battle Monash issued a message to
his corps: 'For the first time in the history of this Corps, all five
Australian divisions will tomorrow engage in the largest and
most important battle operation ever undertaken by this Corps.
They will be supported by an exceptionally powerful artillery
and by tanks and aeroplanes on a scale never previously
attempted. The full resources of our sister Dominion, the Canadian Corps, will also operate on our right, while two British
divisions will guard our left flank … I earnestly wish every soldier of the Corps the best of good fortune, and a glorious and
decisive victory, the story of which will re-echo throughout the
world, and will live for ever in the history of our homeland.'

The battle of Amiens began with the artillery bombard-
ment at 4.20 a.m., 8 August 1918; the first phase went
entirely to plan; the second phase began at 8.20 a.m. And by
1.30 p.m. the third phase was completed. Everything had
moved like clockwork, except in the north where British 3rd
Corps was held up on Chipilly Spur. On one hot summer day
the Australians had taken the enemy gun line — 173 guns —
and 8,000 prisoners and penetrated nearly ten kilometres,
suffering only 2,000 casualties. German defences had been
swept aside along a twenty-kilometre front, with no enemy
capacity to launch a counter-offensive. Ahead of the advancing
armies lay open country before they would reach the Hinden-
burg Line, Germany's last defensive system. 'The Canadians
have done splendidly and the Aussies even better — I am full of
admiration for these corps,' Rawlinson wrote. Amiens was, and
remained, a model of how a battle should be fought.

As Ludendorff related in his memoirs: 'August 8th was
the black day of the German Army in the history of the war.
This was the worst experience I had to go through … The
8th of August opened the eyes of the Staff on both sides; mine
were certainly opened … The Emperor told me later on, after
the failure of the July offensive and after August 8th, he knew
the war could no longer be won.'

France 11 August, 1918

I snatch a few minutes late in the evening to give you
brief particulars of an exceptionally interesting day.

Villers-Bretonneux is a rather large village standing
on a high hill and commanding a view in every direction. That is why it was so important for us to recapture
it away back in April and it was from it that we launched

the great attack of 8 August, which has been so brilliantly successful and which has carried our front line
some ten miles eastward, thus entirely disengaging
Amiens from any danger of capture. Villers-Bretonneux
is now the headquarters of the 1st Australian Division,
while the 2nd Australian Division has its headquarters
on the western outskirts of it.

During this forenoon I was busy at Bertangles (my
headquarters) all the morning preparing plans for a further advance. I was much interrupted by visitors. Quite
early I had a call from Mr Winston Churchill, Minister
of Munitions, and at eleven o'clock, according to
arrangements, I received a call from Field-Marshal Sir
Douglas Haig, who came formally to thank me for the
work done …

We had scarcely started when still three more
motor cars arrived, out of which hopped Monsieur
Clemenceau, the Prime Minister of France, Marshal
Foch, and the French Minister for Finance.

This completed the gathering, met literally by
chance on the actual battlefield and on a site which will
live for ever in Australian history. I suppose that it rarely
happens that such a distinguished gathering should so
meet under such stirring surroundings, with the guns
thundering all around.

France, 14 August 1918

His Majesty the King visited the Australian Corps on
the afternoon of 12 August. The whole function from
first to last has been liberally photographed by the Australian official photographer, and, in due course, I hope

to be able to send you copies of these photographs: but it usually takes several weeks before we can get them passed by the censor and prepared for distribution ...

The King arrived not much after the appointed time in a single car, and I met him at the main gate with my chief of staff and chief administrative officer (Brigadier-Generals Blamey and Carruthers) ... On one side of the main steps were arranged my divisional commanders and the other generals of my staff, while on the other side were ranged about sixty of the junior officer members of my staff. The clerical staff of corps headquarters were all accommodated in the upper windows of the chateau, looking out over the scene. I then presented my divisional commanders and the King chatted for a few minutes with each.

A square of carpet had been arranged in the centre of the piazza and on it stood a small table, a footstool, and a drawn sword. The King then had my name called and I stepped up before him and, at his behest, knelt and received the accolade of knighthood, and, when he had bidden me rise, he presented me with the insignia of a Knight Commander of the Bath. He shook hands most warmly and made me a little speech, commending my work and that of the Australian troops.

Subsequently the King walked around with me and inspected the battle trophies, and, shortly after, his motor car drew up in front of the steps and, with a cordial farewell, he drove away between the cheering ranks of the troops.

The whole ceremony lasted only half an hour, and took place amid brilliant sunshine, and with our

Australian Squadron aeroplanes circling overhead.

France, 15 August 1918

During the operations which commenced on 8 August, the Australian Corps captured a number of enemy head-quarters, both divisional and corps. The whole of the headquarters of the 51st German Army Corps was cap-tured intact, with all their papers, paraphernalia, motor cars, and gear complete.

Amongst the spoil gathered up in this headquarters was a box containing one hundred Iron Crosses all ready for issue. They were in due course 'issued' to our own 'Biljims' who came back from the battle wearing Iron Crosses all over their anatomy.

I send you by post herewith under separate cover one of these Iron Crosses, together with a piece of the ribbon belonging to it. The amount of spoil captured, both in quantity and variety, is simply beyond descrip-tion, and the troops have stuffed their pockets with all sorts of interesting souvenirs.

France, 21 August 1918

During the present series of operations the captures made by the Australian Corps exceed everything in the previous records of the war. Our total prisoners closely approaches 10,000 and among them are represented more than seventy-five different units of the German Army ...

In this battle we captured no fewer than five regi-mental commanders. This was due to the great depth of our penetration (thirteen miles) and to the rapidity with which my plan was carried out ...

You may wonder that I did not sent you any cable, or that I do not now send you a graphic description of the battles – but the whole thing has been too stupendous, and I have been far too busy to attempt any such thing. The greater part of each day is occupied in the planning of fresh offensives and holding conferences with my divisional commanders. Today the 1st Division and the 32nd British Division carried out an operation for the capture of Herleville and Chuignolles – quite a respectable operation, about twice the size of the battle of Hamel.

After hard fighting Lihons fell on 11 August, and on 21 August the Third Army and Fourth Army together launched an offensive along a fifty-kilometre front, the Third Army recapturing Albert the next day. Monash pressed the 3rd Division forward to drive the Germans back over the Somme. On 29 August his men reached the Somme where the river bends and marshes begin. Monash determined to take the fortified height dominating the old walled city of Péronne, Mont St Quentin, using a weary brigade of 2nd Division. He was pushing his men hard but was determined to maintain the initiative. On 31 August the Australians stormed the slopes of Mont St Quentin after a brilliant artillery bombardment, and gained a foothold, holding it against heavy enemy counter-attacks. Monash ordered them reinforced by 6th, 7th and 14th Brigades, forcing the latter to make a ten-hour march. 'I was compelled to harden my heart,' Monash late wrote, 'and to insist that it was imperative to recognize a great opportunity and seize it unflinchingly.' The Australians stormed the summit on 1 September. Rawlinson heard Monash's news of its capture with disbelief and described its seizure as one of the finest feats of the war. Péronne fell on 3 September, forcing an enemy retreat to the Hindenburg Line, twenty kilometres distant, where the last battles of the war would be fought.

France, 8 September 1918

[I enclose a cutting] from the *Morning Post* of 2 September, containing an account of our capture of Mont St Quentin. This feat is described throughout the English press as the greatest single feat of arms in the war, and I am sure that it will live to become a classic in military literature. It followed a swift turning movement at night, on the lines of some of 'Stonewall' Jackson's sudden onslaughts, but of course, on a very much larger scale. This capture of Péronne has had a decisive influence upon the course of the campaign.

I am so sorry that I am quite unable to find time to give you any account of the fighting of the last four weeks. It seems to me extraordinary that it is only a month today since we commenced the great Allied counter-offensive. No one could have foreseen the extraordinary success which was going to result, and in one short month the whole prospects of the war have been changed and the end has come appreciably nearer.

France, 11 September 1918

I am again shifting my headquarters today, and this generally means the temporary disorganization of the whole of my offices, and several hours during which I am unable to carry on my ordinary routine work. I seize the present opportunity, therefore, to write you in reply to recent letters and about current affairs.

This is the third move of my headquarters since our counter-offensive opened on 8 August. The factor that controls our moves is the length of our telephone communications. As the battle moves forward brigades and also divisions have to move forward with it, and finally also corps and army. If my headquarters thereby falls back more than five or six miles behind the division, the maintenance of communication by telegraph and telephone becomes very difficult and inconvenient, besides being a great burden to the signals staff to maintain all the lines in good working order. Our advance has been so rapid, and our series of victories so decisive that every few days the whole question has to be reconsidered. I moved first from Bertangles to Glisy and then from Glisy to Méricourt. In the latter place I have inhabited, for the past ten days, the ruins of a chateau which, only a week before I got into it, had been inhabited by the enemy. I have scarcely got settled down in it when I have to move forward another ten miles, this time into a hutted camp which I have had built in the wreckage of a little wood in the middle of the devastated area overlooking Péronne. My front line is already another ten miles east of this latter point and we are close up to the Hindenburg Line ...

The question of the adequate recognition of the work done in the war by Australian troops, and indeed by all Dominion troops of the Empire, is a very burning one. Far from it being the case that Dominion troops have in the past received more than their fair share of recognition, the exact contrary is the case. For some time past the German propaganda has been trying to represent Lloyd George as climbing to victory over the corpses of Canadians and Australians and putting them in where ever the fighting has been hottest. The Imperial Government and also G.H.Q. have been rather afraid of the effect of such propaganda, and they have rather erred on the side of unduly suppressing references to the deeds of the Australians. In connection with the present counter-offensive the London Press started very badly, and, in fact, in several striking instances attributed successes achieved by the Australians to other troops who had previously failed in the same tasks. I made a very serious remonstration about this to Perry Robinson of *The Times*, to Rawlinson, to Lawrence, and to the Chief of the Imperial General Staff, Sir Henry Wilson, telling them plainly that my own appeal to my troops was the prestige of Australian arms, and that, unless the performances of the Australians were justly placarded, I would not hold myself responsible for the maintenance of their fighting spirit. I put it plainly that they are by nature and instinct sportsmen, and that they would refuse to go on playing any game in which their scores were not put up on the scoring-board. These remonstrations have had an astonishingly successful result, because a complete change has come over the scene, and, as you will see by the very large number of cuttings I have recently sent you, the London Press has latterly given us quite generous recognition.

The best troops of the United Kingdom have long ago been used up and we now have a class of man who is without initiative or individuality. They are brave enough, but are simply unskilful. They would be all right if properly led, but their officers, particularly the junior officers, are poor young men from the professions and from office stools in the English cities, who have had no experience whatever of independent responsibility or leadership. Very few English divisions can today be classed as first-class fighting troops, relied upon to carry out the tasks set. On the other hand, the Canadians and Australians have never failed to achieve all their objectives strictly according to plan ...

Marshal Foch had ordered a massive offensive along the entire Western Front that would hopefully carry the Allied armies to the Rhine and into Germany's heartland in the early months of 1919. The offensives would begin on 26 September from the Flanders front in the north to Alsace-Lorraine in the south, where Pershing's American army was now concentrated in strength. The last and vital blow, to break the Hindenburg Line which ran more than ten kilometres deep from Cambrai in the north to Laon, just past St Quentin in the south, would be launched on 27 September 1918 by Byng's Third Army and on 29 September on Byng's southern flank by Rawlinson's Fourth Army, of which Australian Corps was the spearhead.

Attacking the Hindenburg Line was a formidable undertaking. All the troops were weary, none more so than the Australians, understrength and in almost constant action since late March. Monash was exhausted. Blamey was concerned about his Chief's health. Monash was drawn, almost haggard — his weight was down to 75 kilos (around 11.5 stone); he would be seen driving past in his staff car, visiting his divisions, 'for long periods in silence', deep in thought. On the eve of battle Prime Minister Hughes ordered Monash to organise the repatriation of original Anzacs: this was followed by orders to disband eight battalions, seven of them 'went on strike' rather than disband. On 18 September 1st and 4th Divisions entered their last battle – and victory – of the war, storming the Hindenburg Line's outer defences, the Outpost Line, and were withdrawn for rest.

Monash's corps was now down to three divisions, a meagre resource with which to crack open the three defence lines that formed the Hindenburg system. Rawlinson informed Monash that he would have under his command two fresh American divisions that could be deployed in the initial attack to capture the first two lines, leaving the Australians to follow them and secure the third. There would be no creeping barrage, for the fighting would be close, but tanks would be used and both smoke shells and mustard gas would be fired to assist the Americans in the initial attack

France, 27 September 1918

I commenced today a series of decisive battle operations. About a fortnight ago I prepared a plan for a 'break through' the Hindenburg Line, but stipulated that this was not possible with my own resources, owing to the fact that the 1st and 4th Divisions had in my opinion done as much fighting in the recent past as it was fair to ask them, and I insisted upon them being given a long rest in a back area.(This has since been acceded to.) This left me only the 2nd, 3rd and 5th Divisions, and was, in my opinion, not sufficient strength in infantry to carry out the undertaking. I therefore stipulated for two strong divisions to assist, and as a result about a week ago I had added to my resources two American divisions, viz., the 27th and 30th. These are strong divisions and the men are of a very fine quality, although the commanders and staffs are quite inexperienced.

I thereupon drew up a detailed plan for a large operation extending over several days, and this has been adopted in its entirety by the Fourth Army Commander and the Commander-in-Chief. I have been engaged for the last six days in developing and perfecting the plan and holding a series of conferences to carry it into effect. It has been a very strenuous and anxious time. Today was the first occasion when I have had even a few moments' leisure …

From now on for the next forty-eight hours I undertake the heavy artillery bombardment of the St Quentin canal and the main Hindenburg Line with over a thousand guns of all calibres. The two American divisions will attack on the morning of 29 September and, if all goes well, I shall during the afternoon push through the whole of the 3rd and 5th Australian Divisions with all their artillery and technical troops to exploit their success and shall follow this up with the 2nd Australian Division two or three days after. My immediate objective is the important railway junction of Busigny …

Monash makes little mention in letters of his last battle. It came close to being a disaster, and was saved only by the fortitude of the Australian troops. The American attack, which began at dawn, 29 September, fell apart in the first hours, failing to seize even the First Line, and 2nd, 3rd and 5th Divisions had to fight the battle from scratch, storming the last fortified village, Montbrehain, on 5 October. It was a great victory and was the last action fought by Australian troops on the Western Front. On that day the Australians were withdrawn for rest and regrouping and Monash took a fortnight's leave.

On the same day Germany's new Chancellor, Prince Max of Baden, notified American President Wilson, that Germany would accept an armistice on the basis of Wilson's 'Fourteen Points'; Wilson replied that Germany must discuss armistice terms with Marshal Foch, the Commander-in-Chief of the Allied armies.

France, 3 November 1918

On 18 October I cabled: 'Created by King Albert Grand Officer de L'Order de la Couronne Belgium. Monash.'

You will also be very pleased to hear that I have in addition to the above, also been awarded during the last week the French *Croix de Guerre* with Palm Leaf.

France, 3 November 1918

Paul and I crossed to London on 6 October, visiting General Birdwood at his headquarters, about a hundred miles away from my own, on the way to Boulogne. The crossing and journey to London were quite uneventful.

I was principally occupied during the first week in giving sittings to Longstaff, which is a very tiring and boring business. However, he has now practically finished the three-quarter length sitting portrait of me, which is intended for you, and I regard it as a very great success, and those who have seen it admire it greatly. He also commenced a large painting for the Sydney National Gallery, which is taken full length, the figure standing in the open with a background of the desolation of war all around. Longstaff has gone to a very great deal of trouble and had a photographer along to take me in about thirty different poses. He would not pose me himself but insisted that I should adopt quite a number of different natural, habitual poses; he merely corrected quite minor details as to the position of the hands and feet, etc. ...

Another very interesting trip which took a whole day was when I called for Lady Forrest at her hotel and motored her about fifty miles out of London, to Cobham Hall in Kent, where the Countess of Darnley has allowed part of her beautiful Elizabethan home to be used as a convalescent home for some forty Australian officers. Lady Forrest and I spent several hours chatting with the patients and the nursing staff, and then lunched with the Darnleys. I remember the Countess quite well as Florence Morphy of Benalla (or was it Beechworth?) The Earl is a very fine man still and reminiscent of his athletic days. You will doubtless remember him as the Honourable Ivo Bligh, who brought out to Australia the cricket team which was the first to lose the rubber against Australia, giving rise to the expression in vogue at the time that he and his team would only be able to carry back to England the *ashes* of English cricket, which had been cremated in the fire of Australian prowess. The Earl showed me, on his writing-table, a tiny little urn under a glass cover, which the Australian ladies had given him at the time, and which is supposed to contain the 'ashes'.

France, 8 November 1918

The negotiations for peace, opened by the Germans on 7 October, have dragged their weary way along for over a month, during which time the Australian Corps has been resting in a beautiful area in the valley of the Somme lying between Amiens and Abbeville, and my own headquarters has been established in the village of Eu, near the coast, at the mouth of the Somme, close to the famous watering-place, Le Treport. I am myself with my headquarters officers inhabiting an annex to the chateau of the Comte d'Eu, the younger brother of the Prince of Orleans, who also lives here when not in England. I have just received word that the German armistice delegates have passed through our lines at Guise and were entertained last night at dinner by General Debeney of the First French Army, and that they are this morning being sent on by special train to receive from Marshal Foch the agreed-upon conditions of armistice.

In case they do not at once accept, it is the intention to go on hammering the enemy, who is now very badly disorganized and very nearly driven out of occupied France. To meet this contingency, my corps is again moving up into the line. The 1st Division commenced to move last night, the 4th Division commences to entrain to-night, the corps headquarters gets under way the day after to-morrow. The remaining divisions stay in this area until I require them. If, on the other hand, the armistice conditions are accepted, about which I myself feel fairly sanguine, I have no doubt that my corps will be employed as part of the army of occupation, and it is quite on the cards that, within a very few days or weeks from now, I shall be on German soil in military charge of a considerable slice of Germany ...

On 27 October Turkey had sued for an armistice. Its armies had collapsed in Syria under Allenby's mid-September offensive and its Balkan front fell apart simultaneously with the defeat of Bulgaria. One week later Austria-Hungary sued for peace terms. Stripped of allies, and racked by revolution, Germany signed an armistice at Foch's headquarters on 11 November 1918.

France, 12 November, 1918

The march into Germany has already commenced.

I left Eu yesterday morning by motor, and journeyed 120 miles to Le Cateau [over the frontier in Belgium] where I have temporarily established my headquarters. The journey took me across the whole length of our battlefields from Villers-Bretonneux to here (Le Cateau), passing the formidable and forbidding desert of eighty odd miles devastated by the war. Le Cateau is on the fringe of the territory which has barely been touched by fighting, and every mile takes one more and more into the country which more nearly resembles English pasture land, with hedgerows and woods.

The chateau which I now occupy had as its last occupant Prince Rupprecht of Bavaria, he who was to marry the Luxembourg Princess. It is spacious and still has most of its furniture more or less intact, though war-worn. All the tapestries and the pictures have, however, been stolen, and most of the plate-glass mirrors in the beautiful state-rooms have been used for revolver prac-tice. As most of the glass in the windows of the chateau has gone it is rather cold and cheerless. It is from the same chateau that Lord French in 1914 fought the battle of Mons.

The town, which is about the size of Warrnam-bool, is crammed full of British troops, in process of being organized for the march into Germany. There are captured enemy guns everywhere, and the roads are blocked with our own guns, the lighter pieces moving forward and the heavier ones being taken back. There is an endless stream of motor lorries on every road.

Of my five divisions the 1st is already moved up into close proximity and the 4th is in process of moving up by train. However, the move has been much delayed by the explosion of delay action mines at various railway stations *en route*; but it is one of the conditions of the armistice that the enemy has to disclose the location of all these mines. He has today done so, and his engi-neer officers are helping us at various places to find and uncharge them. Some of these mines have been blown in territory which he has vacated for over six weeks, so that their action must have been due to the employment of a corrosive acid eating away a safety device in the fuse, an extraordinary prostitution of sci-entific ingenuity.

Under the terms of the armistice the enemy has

been allowed fifteen days to evacuate Belgium and Lux-embourg to his frontier, and another fifteen days to evacuate all the German territory west of the Rhine. The total distance we shall have to go from here to the Rhine is nearly 200 miles, measuring along the roads and railways we shall have to take.

Our troops are to follow him up at a one-day interval and a mixed armistice commission has started work today at Spa, the late German general headquarters, to define the position of the respective armies at the end of each day's march. Any of his troops which we find on our side of these delimitation lines will be made prisoners of war.

Our march into Germany will be a stupendous and difficult operation, owing to the lack of good roads, paucity of railways and the entire absence of supplies in the territories which we will occupy. Every scrap of what we require must be carried with us and there is very little hope that the roads and railways can be opened up as rapidly as the troops can advance ...

Naturally everybody in France is in the highest spirits. All the little villages and larger towns, even those which are now a mere heap of bricks, are bedecked with flags of all colours, and the emaciated and careworn villagers who have been for four years under enemy dominion are at last wreathed in happy smiles. The country is, however, absolutely denuded of supplies, and such things as vegetables, eggs, milk and comforts of that kind, are not to be had. The problem of supply so far away from the coast is going to be a particularly difficult one, as the railways are very congested. However, as the enemy has to hand over to us at once 5,000 locomotives, and something like 100,000 railway wagons, the situation should in a little while be much relieved.

London, 20 November 1918

I find myself unexpectedly in London, having been telegraphed for by Mr Hughes two days ago, to come over to confer with him on questions of Reconstruction, Repatriation, and Demobilization.

Mr Hughes seems to have now definitely made up his mind that I am to take entire responsible charge of the process of demobilization, on behalf of the Commonwealth and the A.I.F. After full consultation with General Birdwood and General White I have come to the conclusion that my only possible course of action is to place myself, unreservedly and unconditionally at the disposal of the Government. Mr Hughes's idea is to appoint me with some such title as 'Director-General of Demobilization' and as the head of a Special Board or Department composed of both soldiers and civilians. Whether this department will be a quite independent one directly under Mr Hughes as Minister representing the Government, or will remain for some time under the G.O.C., A.I.F., is a point that has still to be settled. Generals Birdwood and White and I will have a special conference in London with the Prime Minister tomorrow to settle the whole plan – they having also just arrived from France for this purpose.

I would have to relinquish the command of the corps almost immediately. The fighting is over, and there is nothing further to be gained by sitting down on the Rhine for several months with nothing particular to do. Moreover, I have good reasons to suspect that, if the Armistice works smoothly, as it has every appearance of doing, only two or at most three divisions of the corps will after all be allowed to go into Germany – perhaps only one division.

London, 28 December 1918

I should like to tell you something of the State Banquet last night at Buckingham Palace, to which I was invited. Apart from the Royal family, President and Mrs Wilson and their suite, the members of the King's and Queen's Households, and the Ambassadors, the guests numbered in all about sixty-eight persons. It was a very special privilege to be present, particularly in view of the historic occasion ...

Each guest was first welcomed by the King, and by him presented to President Wilson, who stood on his right, then welcomed by the Queen and presented to Mrs Wilson. When each guest had passed he was ushered along a brilliantly-lighted corrridor, full of beautiful paintings, into the Banquet Hall, which was a blaze of splendour such as, I imagine, has seldom been seen before. In size it was about as wide and half as long as the Ball Room of Government House in Melbourne; richly decorated in white and gold, with six great crystal electroliers spreading a magnificent illumination. At one end was the dais and throne (which remained unoccupied throughout the evening) and at the other end an organ gallery, accommodating the band of the Royal Regiment of Artillery. The whole corridor and the whole of the Banquet Hall were lined on all sides with bearded Yeomen of the Guard, in their traditional Tudor black, gold, and crimson, standing at attention, with their pikes and halberds, throughout the whole banquet. In addition all the table attendants were in the royal livery, scarlet and gold, there being one to each guest, standing stiffly at attention behind his chair. The chairs were crimson damask with white and gold frames.

The royal gold plate had been brought from Windsor Castle, and made a most amazingly magnificent display. The table appointments, including plates, knife-handles, forks, spoons, salt-cellars, flower-bowls, vases and dishes were all of solid gold, highly polished and brilliantly scintillating. Each flower-bowl was a beautiful specimen of delicate modelling, and most of them were large and imposing. The flowers throughout were scarlet and crimson, comprising chiefly azaleas and ranunculi. Around three sides of the hall were displayed great high trophies of the remainder of the Royal gold plate, trays, dishes, vases and salvers, each most exquis-itely modelled and chased, and each specially illuminated by concealed electric globes so that their polished surfaces reflected a blaze of golden light in all directions. On the walls were also three of the famous Royal Tapestries.

Except the small handful of naval and military offi-cers, the guests were in evening-dress (not Court dress), all wearing the stars and ribbons of their orders and miniatures of their badges. The ladies were in full evening toilette, with diamond coronets and necklaces.

As soon as all the guests had taken their appointed

places at the table, which was arranged in one great horse-shoe, the Royal party entered, ushered in by the Officers of the Household, walking backwards and waving their hands. The President led in the Queen, the King followed with Mrs Wilson, and then came the rest of the royal family. As the small procession entered the hall the band played a fanfare, followed by 'The Star-Spangled Banner' and 'God Save the King'. It was a most impressive and historic moment, after which all at once sat down and dinner was promptly served.

I had on my right Rudyard Kipling, and beyond him Sir Joseph Thomson (President of the Royal Society), and on my left Lord Burnham (proprietor of the *Daily Telegraph*):, whom I had entertained at my headquarters in France last September, and beyond him, Sir Henry Wilson. Opposite to me were Louis Botha, J.S. Sargent (the painter) and Winston Churchill. The meal passed amid buzz of conversation and laughter, and without restraint of any kind. Contrary to custom, the two toasts came on before and not after the dessert, and before the port was served. When the King rose to speak, the whole company, including the ladies, rose also, and remained standing while the King delivered his oration, and until President Wilson had completed his reply. The speeches were brief, but dignified in tone and lofty in sentiment, and Wilson's mobile face and hands were a study to watch. Cigars and cigarettes were served at the table, but the ladies did not leave alone, being conducted by their cavaliers straight into the Red Drawing Room, all the guests following. All the men smoked there, and coffee was served. Here three groups were formed, respectively round the King, the Queen, and President and Mrs Wilson, and most of the guests were presented to each in turn. I had just five minutes with the King and the President; but over ten minutes with the Queen, who talked about her son now at Australian Corps Headquarters, and was most enthusiastic in praise of Australia and her soldiers, many of whom she had met at Windsor Castle. I also had a chat with the young and beautiful Duchess of Sutherland (whom I had already met a couple of weeks ago at the Godleys), and who was 'on duty' as Mistress of the Robes. The Queen wore cloth of gold and many magnificent diamonds, especially on the corsage, including the Koh-i-noor and the great Cullinan. My five minutes with the President were quite formal. He has a smile not unlike Roosevelt.

The King and Queen withdrew precisely at midnight, and then the distinguished company dispersed.

Epilogue

Monash was appointed GCMG, a high honour awarded previously to only two Australians, and received honours from France, Belgium and the United States, but nothing from Australia. Charged with the task of organizing the repatriation of the AIF, he set up offices in London where he was joined early in 1919 by his wife and daughter. He rode on horseback at the head of the Australian troops in the Anzac Day parade in London and led the Australian contingent in the great Victory Parade in July 1919. In August, feeling that the role played in the war by Australian troops was still barely known or in danger of being forgotten, he began writing *The Australian Victories in France in 1918*, and finished the book in four weeks. It was published in 1920 and reprinted several times.

Monash and his family returned to Australia in December 1919. He had hopes of appointment to a position of national importance but this was denied him. In August 1920 he was appointed general manager and later chairman of Victoria's State Electricity Commission on a salary of 3,000 pounds a year, resigning all the directorates that might have conflicted with his new duties and responsibilities. He threw himself into his new job. The SEC was formed to exploit the brown coal reserves in Gippsland to provide electricity for the people of Victoria. Its first steps included the takeover of existing electricity companies, the expansion of the open-cut mine at Yallourn and the construction not only of a powerhouse but a complete town there, and the erection of transmission towers throughout the state. Monash supervised every aspect of construction, as was only to be expected, and workers found him little different from the man the Diggers knew — approachable and human. One of his employees recalled how Monash would talk to anyone on the train journeys to Yallourn — 'the sort of man who would encourage anybody … You could talk to him as though he was your father. He was a very good listener; gave you the impression that you were a most important person.' The Yallourn powerhouse was turned on in 1924 and the SEC was showing a profit in 1927.

Monash's wife died from cancer in 1920 and he devoted himself to his daughter Bertha, who married Gershon Bennett, a successful Melbourne dentist, in 1921. He liked and admired his son-in-law and doted on the four children born to the marriage; he continued to take solicitous care of many of his relatives and was particularly close to his unmarried sister Mat. When the dignified widower attended the races in Melbourne with Lizzie Bentwich, a former friend of his wife and himself, gossip began but soon came to an end. Monash was a man who needed companionship. His personal prestige remained high, higher than that of perhaps any other Australian public figure.

Monash's last years were happy ones. His library reflected his deep interest in history, science and literature; he was broad-minded and nothing shocked him. His music and his gramophone records of Bach, Beethoven, Wagner, Mozart, Mendelssohn, Haydn, were his supreme consolation. He became honorary vice-chancellor of the University of Melbourne in 1923 and President of the Australian Association for the Advancement of Science in 1924. He led Melbourne's Anzac Day march in the following year, when the anniversary became an official day of remembrance in Victoria. In the same year he began observing Yom Kippur – apart from the fasting – but rarely attended worship. He was pleased to be made full general along with Chauvel; they were the first Australians to reach that high rank. As Australia's economic position worsened and the political scene became poisoned with the onset of the 1930s depression he was seen by many as the nation's saviour, the strong man who could lead the nation out of its ills, but he rejected the notion of entering politics.

On 29 September 1931 Sir John Monash suffered a heart attack at his home in Toorak and a series of strokes in the following days; and then pneumonia set in. He died in the morning of 8 October 1931. He was sixty-six.

His body lay in state in the Queen's Hall, Parliament House, Melbourne, with a military guard. His funeral procession to Brighton cemetery on Sunday 11 October was the largest ever witnessed in Australia and a hushed crowd of a quarter of a million people assembled to pay their respects to his memory. Preceded by thousands of ex-servicemen, the bands playing the 'Dead March', his body was borne on a gun-carriage with military escort, his charger following, with boots reversed in the stirrups in tribute to a fallen warrior; aircraft flew overhead and minute guns sounded in salute. The store-keeper's son was buried like a king.

The Governor-General (Sir Isaac Isaacs) said: 'With all Australia I mourn the loss of one of her ablest, bravest, and noblest sons, a loyal servant of King and country. He served Australia and the Empire well, and in his passing he has left an example that will be a beacon light of patriotic and unselfish endeavour.'

★

Apart from Allenby no Allied army commander emerged from the Great War with a reputation as an inspired 'Great Captain', one whose campaigns would be studied with benefit by students of war. Haig's generals were mainly faceless men, who took their rewards when all was over and disappeared, little mourned, into private life. The war had been a grim destroyer of lives but no enhancer of military reputations. Monash, though commanding only a corps, is one of the few exceptions.

He was as successful in planning his battles as in winning them. He was generous – like Montgomery in a later war – in attributing to his soldiers the key to his success and he earned their devotion. In his men Monash was fortunate. He pointed out with pride that his five Australian divisions, comprising just 9.5 per cent of British divisional strength on the Western Front, took during their six months of almost constant action from 27 March to 5 October, 2.42 times the number of enemy prisoners as the average British division, 2.24 times the amount of territory and 2.47 times the number of guns. Monash's divisions suffered 21,243 casualties in this period, 5,000 of whom were killed.

His letters show the pride he felt in his soldiers and his pleasure in their nature. He looked on them like a proud father. 'Success depended primarily upon the military proficiency of the Australian private soldier and his glorious spirit of heroism,' Monash wrote in *The Australian Victories in France in 1918*. 'The democratic institutions under which he was reared, the advanced system of education by which he was trained – teaching him to think for himself and to apply what he had been taught to practical ends – the instinct of sport and adventure which is his national heritage, his pride in his young country, and the opportunity which came to him of creating a great national tradition, were all factors which made him what he was.

'Physically the Australian Army was composed of the flower of the youth of the continent. A volunteer army – the only purely volunteer army that fought in the Great War – it was composed of men carefully selected according to high physical standard ...

'Mentally, the Australian soldier was well endowed. In him there was a curious blend of a capacity for independent judgement with a readiness to submit to self-effacement in a common cause ... Psychologically,

he was easy to lead but difficult to drive. His imagination was readily fired. War was to him a game, and he
played for the side with enthusiasm. His bravery was
founded upon his sense of duty to his unit, comradeship
to his fellows, emulation to uphold his traditions, and a
combative spirit to avenge his hardships and sufferings
upon the enemy. Taking him all in all, the Australian
soldier was, when once understood, not difficult to
handle. But he required a sympathetic handling, which
appealed to his intelligence and satisfied his instinct for
a "square deal".'

Monash dismissed criticism made of the Australians' lack of discipline, explaining that discipline is
after all a means to an end. 'The Australian Army is a
proof that individualism is the best and not the worst
foundation upon which to build up collective discipline.
The Australian is accustomed to team work ... The rela-
tions between the officers and men of the Australian
Army were also of a nature which is deserving of
notice ... there was no officer caste, no social distinction
in the whole force.'

BIBLIOGRAPHY

Cutlack, F.M. (Editor): *War Letters of General Monash* (Angus & Robertson, Sydney, 1934)

Monash, J.: T*he Australian Victories in France in 1918* (Hutchinson, London, 1920)

Serle, Geoffrey: *John Monash: A Biography* (Melbourne University Press, Melbourne, 1982)

Pedersen, Peter: *Monash as Military Commander* (Melbourne University Press, Melbourne, 1985)

Smithers, A.J.: *Sir John Monash* (Cassell, London, 1973)